Urban Wildlife Habitats

Wildlife Habitats

Milton W. Weller, Series Editor

Wildlife Habitats • Volume 3

Urban Wildlife Habitats

A Landscape Perspective

Lowell W. Adams

University of Minnesota Press
Minneapolis
London

Published by the University of Minnesota Press
111 Third Avenue South, Suite 290, Minneapolis, MN 55401-2520
Printed in the United States of America on acid-free paper
Second Printing, 1995

Library of Congress Cataloging-in-Publication Data

Adams, Lowell W.
    Urban wildlife habitats : a landscape perspective / Lowell W.
    Adams.
        p.   cm. – (Wildlife habitats ; v. 3)
    Includes bibliographical references and index.
    ISBN 0-8166-2212-4 (hc : alk. paper). – ISBN 0-8166-2213-2
(pbk. : alk. paper)
        1. Urban ecology (Biology)   2. Nature conservation.   3. Wildlife
    management.   I. Title.   II. Series.
QH541.5.C6A52   1994
333.95'16'091732–dc20   93-44211

To Daniel L. Leedy, mentor and friend

The University of Minnesota Press
gratefully acknowledges
the generous assistance provided
for the publication of this book
by the
Margaret W. Harmon Fund
dedicated
to the publication of books that promote an
understanding and conservation
of our natural resources

Contents

Preface

Historical interest in wildlife conservation and management in North America has focused on game species in rural and wilderness environments. Indeed, the foundation of the wildlife management profession is so rooted. The first wildlife textbook, written by pioneer conservationist Aldo Leopold in 1933, was titled *Game Management.* The logic of this emphasis rests on the fact that game species were of primary importance to people as a source of food during early settlement of the continent and that the human population was small and scattered across the countryside. With advances in agriculture, most North Americans today are no longer dependent on wild game for food, and most of us now live in the city rather than the country.

People have carried their interest in wildlife to the city, and in fairly recent history some effort has focused on wildlife and habitat conservation there. Early thought was given to urban areas by far-sighted individuals, dating back to the 1930s and 1940s, but it was not until the late 1960s and the 1970s that the greatest initial concentration of energy was devoted to the subject. At that time, a number of professional wildlife biologists voiced concern that urban areas were being ignored by the profession. They began pointing out that urban habitats, although highly modified, could support a diversity of wildlife species if appropriately managed. In 1966, Raymond Dasmann, a prominent wildlife biologist, delivered a speech to colleagues in Bowie, Maryland. He discussed "old conservation," concerned mainly with quantity of natural resources, and "new conservation," dealing primarily with clean air and water, open space, outdoor recreation, and quality of the human environment, particularly the urban environment, where most people live (Dasmann 1966). Dr. Dasmann pointed out that generations of humans were growing up in cities, with no roots in the land and little experience in the natural world. He felt that the wildlife profession was too closely identified with game animals and hunters and was too narrow-minded. Dasmann stated that more wildlife biologists should "get out of the woods and into the cities. They must work with city and metropolitan regional planners, with landscape architects and all others concerned with the urban environment to make the cities and metropolitan regions, the places where people live, into environments where each person's everyday life will be enriched to the maximum extent possible by contact with living things and natural beauty."

This book focuses on wildlife and habitats of urban and urbanizing environments. Unlike the rural countryside, such areas are densely populated by people and land unit sizes are small, with multiple ownerships. Even so, many species can inhabit our cities, towns, and villages. Generally, somewhat different management practices are needed and I review these here. The discussion includes game species and nongame species, and invertebrates such as butterflies as well as vertebrates such as birds and mammals. My primary emphasis is on terrestrial species. I have argued that conservation of wildlife and habitat in urban areas is for human benefit as well as for plant and animal benefit. I have tried to base the book on sound research data without making it too technical for the reader. Many terms are explained or defined in the text; others are listed in a glossary at the back of the volume. The book is written primarily for persons who are interested in furthering their understanding of wildlife ecology and management in the metropolitan environment and who are not professional urban wildlife biologists. This includes students of wildlife conservation or related specialities in natural resources. Urban biologists will be knowledgeable of the subject matter but may find the book a useful review.

Acknowledgments

Study and management of urban habitats and associated wildlife resources have only recently received focused attention by wildlife biologists. I have been privileged to be a part of this pioneering effort, and many of my colleagues have contributed to my understanding and appreciation of urban habitats and the wildlife therein. Most influential have been those contributors to the two national symposia on urban wildlife sponsored by the National Institute for Urban Wildlife and for which I served as program chairman.

I greatly appreciate the guidance and advice provided by Vagn Flyger, Daniel L. Leedy, and Larry W. VanDruff in review of early drafts of this book and in numerous discussions of the subject matter that influenced my thinking. Milton W. Weller, series editor, and Barbara A. Coffin, natural/environmental sciences editor for the University of Minnesota Press provided support, encouragement, and editorial assistance for which I am grateful.

Chapter 1
Wildlife Encounters of the Urban Kind

This little book is about wildlife habitat in the urban environment. Consequently, considerable attention is devoted to "urban wildlife," a term as yet having no clear universal meaning. What is urban wildlife? Over the years I have cataloged three basic stages of public perception. Stage one is what I call the "On-the-Wrong-Track Stage." When asked about urban wildlife, individuals in this category usually say something such as, "Oh yes, urban 'wild life' is the rowdy nightlife of city bars and entertainment establishments on Friday and Saturday nights." The second stage of public perception I call the "On-the-*Right*-Track Stage." Persons here readily associate urban areas with starlings, pigeons, house sparrows, rats, mice, and, yes, cockroaches! The third stage I label the "Enlightened Stage" because these people talk about the wide diversity of nondomestic species that can inhabit our cities, towns, and villages. In considering the diversity of wildlife in the urban environment, one must consider the diversity of habitats. Let's look at a few such habitats.

Human residential dwellings as well as other buildings and structures provide habitat for some species. Of course, few people desire to share their homes with squirrels, raccoons, or bats in the attic, but species such as house sparrows and barn swallows that build their nests in various nooks and crannies and under overhanging eaves on the outside of one's house may be tolerated or even encouraged. Although not readily thought of as "urban wildlife" in North America, the barn swallow is cosmopolitan and closely associated with hu-

1

mans. It is one of the most widespread bird species in the world. Beijing was once known as the "City of Swallows" because of the birds' propensity for nesting in Chinese homes, where they were welcomed (Jackson 1992), probably in no small measure because of the many insects they eat.

Perhaps no bird typifies urban wildlife more than the house sparrow, regarded as a nuisance and pest by some, but more favorably by others. Regardless of one's personal feelings toward the bird, I think that it can be appreciated for its adaptability, which contributes to its success in the urban environment. An example of such adaptability is the bird's ability to open automatic sliding doors. Sparrows at the Hamilton, New Zealand, intercity bus station do this to gain access to food crumbs from tables of a small café within the station. In this case, birds learned how to interrupt the light beams from the sensor mechanism, causing the doors to open. A bird would fly slowly past the "eye" of the sensor, or hover briefly in front of it, or land on top of the sensor box, lean forward and bend its neck until its head triggered the sensor and the door opened (Breitwisch and Breitwisch 1991).

Other species use buildings, too. Twenty-two species of birds have been recorded nesting on the flat roofs of buildings, including gulls, terns, and common nighthawks (Fisk 1978). In addition, the endangered peregrine falcon nests on the ledges (artificial cliffs) and roofs of skyscrapers. Certainly greater use of such structures would result if people more actively managed "rooftop gardens."

Some species, such as the American crow, historically have been considered rural wildlife. But crow nesting and populations appear to be increasing in urban areas (Laux et al. 1991). Like the house sparrow, the crow is resourceful and adaptable, which contributes to its success in exploiting urban habitats. The bird eats a wide variety of food items, including nuts, and at least one California crow has learned how to use automobiles as nutcrackers. A single bird was observed hovering over a busy street in Long Beach where it dropped a palm fruit from its beak. After completing this task, the crow flew to a nearby lamppost and patiently waited for a car to smash the hard outer covering, exposing the fruit, which the bird promptly retrieved and ate. The entire feeding sequence was observed a second time (Grobecker and Pietsch 1978).

Gray squirrels are one of the most common mammals found in urban areas throughout much of North America. These squirrels need some large trees for nesting and for providing food in the form of nuts, but they do not require extensive forest. (Photo: J. M. Hadidian, National Park Service.)

Peccaries (pig-like mammals) also are not typically thought of as "urban wildlife." In some Arizona communities, however, peccaries are finding residential backyards to their liking. The animals are attracted to food, water, and shade. If undisturbed, peccaries will spend much of the hot portions of the day under a nearby shade tree only to venture out to the back porch to empty the pet food dish and then return to their shade tree (W. W. Shaw personal communication 1990).

Other areas, such as cemeteries, provide habitat to wildlife in the urban environment. Ninety-five species of birds have been observed in cemeteries of the Boston metropolitan area (Thomas and Dixon 1974). Starlings, robins, and blue jays are abundant, as are common flickers, song sparrows, catbirds, ring-necked pheasants, and mockingbirds. Twenty species of mammals have been recorded using the cemeteries, including raccoon, striped skunk, red fox, woodchuck, red squirrel, flying squirrel, opossum, muskrat, and cottontail.

Small city parks, if managed with an eye toward wildlife, can provide habitat. Recent efforts were initiated to enhance Toledo Heights Park, in Toledo, Iowa, for wildlife while maintaining the park's recreational functions (City of Toledo, Iowa 1987). Toledo Heights is a 40-acre (16-hectare), city-owned park, and a newly created management plan calls for establishment of a fruit-bearing shrub layer, winter wildlife cover, and more natural areas in portions of the park. Some 1,300 shrubs were planted in 1986-1987, including gray and red-osier dogwood, Amur honeysuckle, chokecherry, and highbush cranberry. In addition, a four-acre (1.6-hectare) native tallgrass prairie is being reestablished with plantings of Indian grass, big bluestem, little bluestem, western wheat grass, sideoats grama, and switchgrass. Other management considerations to benefit wildlife include retaining snag and cavity trees in the naturalized areas and erection of wood duck and bluebird nest boxes. The park was certified as an urban wildlife sanctuary by the National Institute for Urban Wildlife in 1987.

Creative management of school yards can provide play areas for children as well as habitat for wildlife. The Washington Elementary School, in Berkeley, California, provides a good example of what can be done (Schicker 1987). Through the initiative of a local landscape architect and the school principal, and with local community involvement, the Washington Environmental Yard was created. This project diversified a one-and-a-half-acre (0.6-hectare) asphalt play yard into a variety of play and learning environments for the children and, at the same time, improved habitat conditions for wildlife. A half-acre (0.2-hectare) natural resource area—consisting of ponds, wooded areas, and meadows—was developed by completely stripping away all the asphalt. The whole area provides an outdoor classroom for teaching environmental and science education.

There are other habitats of the urban landscape, including aquatic areas such as lakes and ponds. And there are many other wildlife species that can be accommodated if we consider their needs along with our own. I will discuss these in greater detail in coming chapters, but first let's establish a basic ecological foundation from which to proceed.

Chapter 2
Ecological Processes

Before discussing the management of wildlife in cities, towns, and villages, it would be useful to consider some basic ecological principles and processes that are fairly well recognized by ecologists, wildlife biologists, and other natural resources specialists. Our understanding of plants and animals in relation to each other and to their environment in urban areas is by no means complete. Knowledge of ecological principles and processes is important, not only for managing wildlife, but also for understanding the basic influences and constraints placed on human populations.

The Energy Pyramid

Practically all of the energy used by plants and animals on earth comes from the sun. Over the years, and through increasingly sophisticated study, use of energy by plants and animals has become better understood. Green plants capture solar energy and, by also using carbon dioxide and water, manufacture simple sugars and give off water and oxygen in a process called photosynthesis. The simple sugars produced in photosynthesis are the building blocks for more complex carbohydrates, proteins, fats, and other substances that support life. Thus, green plants are nature's food-manufacturing factories (the producers). Some animals feed directly on green plants (and thus are termed herbivores), whereas others (carnivores) feed only on other animals. (Some plants, such as the pitcher plant and the Ve-

5

nus's-flytrap, also are carnivorous.) In addition, some animals are omnivorous, feeding on both plants and animals. These food chains (and more complex food webs) are governed by the flow of energy through the different trophic (feeding) levels.

Some production by green plants is used to sustain their own life; much is available to herbivores. Herbivores, like the green plants below them, use a portion of this converted energy for their own maintenance and reproduction, and some is stored in muscle and other tissue that then may be consumed by carnivores. Thus, at each step up to a higher trophic level in the food chain, less energy is available, so that top predators have only a fraction of energy available to them that was present in the system at the producer level. This process of energy flow through food chains results in a pyramid of energy, with the broad base of the pyramid at the bottom of the chain and the apex at the top. Because of the scarcity of available energy at the top of food chains, predators typically have lower population levels than do organisms below them. Thus, we frequently see a pyramid of numbers in nature that closely resembles the pyramid of energy.

Finally, decomposers, the organisms of decay, play an important role in food chains. These organisms, largely bacteria and fungi, may follow any of the trophic levels. They live on dead material and cause its breakdown and decomposition into basic chemical elements, including carbon, hydrogen, oxygen, nitrogen, iron, and calcium. These elements are recycled in food chains, with the result that most elements in our own bodies were once parts of other living things. Let's examine some simple food chains that might be found in the urban environment.

Urban Food Chains

The terrestrial and aquatic food chains shown in Figure 1 are simplified for purposes of illustration. Even so, they are realistic for many urban areas.

Cottontail rabbits are a common sight in backyards, wooded borders and hedgerows, and other areas of the metropolitan landscape over much of the eastern United States. On the one hand, their role as herbivores is not appreciated by avid gardeners growing lettuce and other green vegetables for the kitchen table! On the other hand, their presence in urban areas brings enjoyment to millions of people.

Figure 1. Energy from the sun moves through ecosystems in pathways called food chains. All life forms are interconnected, and thus interdependent. (Reprinted, by permission of the publisher, from Leedy and Adams 1984.)

One of the better-known facts about cottontails is that they are highly proficient in reproduction. The breeding season typically runs from March to September over most of the rabbit's range. After a gestation period of 25 to 32 days, a litter of three to eight (usually four to five) young is born (Trippensee 1948). Females generally produce two to three litters per season, so a total of 15 young per female per season is not unreasonable. Natural mortality, however, typically results in loss of about 80% of the young by fall. A rural density of over five cottontails per acre (12 per hectare) has been reported (Trippensee 1948), but more typical late summer–early fall densities are on the order of about one rabbit per two acres (1.2 per hectare) (Allen 1962). I am unaware of comparable density figures for metropolitan areas.

The next trophic level in the terrestrial food chain of Figure 1 is represented by the red fox. This fox is more adaptable to suburban living than is its gray cousin. The red fox preys on cottontails, mice, and other small animals, and also feeds on fruits and berries. The female red fox (vixen) cannot match the cottontail in production of young. Vixens produce young at one year of age and only a single litter is born in a breeding season. (Cottontails born early in the season may produce their own young by fall.) After a gestation period of 53 days, a litter of one to nine (average five to six) fox pups is born (Trippensee 1953).

Little research has been conducted on urban foxes in North America, but considerable effort has gone into studying fox population biology and habitat use in metropolitan areas of England. Habitats used by foxes in British towns and cities include railways and yards, private gardens and housing estates, institution grounds of hospitals, colleges, and other schools, cemeteries, nurseries, golf courses, public parks, factories and docks, quarries, and river banks (Kolb 1985). Although densities of foxes vary according to suitability of the habitat and other factors, they typically are much lower than densities of cottontails. The average fox density recently reported for seven English towns was about one fox per 28 acres (11 hectares) (Harris and Rayner 1986). Although this density is much lower than that for cottontails, it is about 18 times higher than the average fox density for an 18-year period (1963-1980) in the rural Prairie Pothole Region of North Dakota (Sargeant et al. 1984).

Food chains also exist in aquatic environments. For example, algae and other minute plant life in urban ponds or lakes are fed on by zooplankton (small animal life) that becomes food for larger animals such as larvae of mayflies, dragonflies, and damselflies. These predaceous aquatic insects are food for small fish such as minnows and bluegill on which larger fish, such as bass, feed. Birds such as osprey, bald eagle, and great blue heron also may be at the top of aquatic food chains. Sometimes, the role of these larger predators is not appreciated. For example, largemouth bass and snapping turtles in an urban impoundment will take newly hatched ducklings, an activity that some residents may find displeasing, especially if they witness the event. However, predation is a part of nature, and predators should not be labeled "bad" or "undesirable" simply because of the role they play in the food chain.

As a group, natural predators are lacking in urban areas (and frequently are lacking in rural areas as well). These animals were maligned and often killed by people in the past, but there are signs that the public is becoming more understanding of their role in nature. Some predators (for example, the peregrine falcon) are even being reintroduced into the urban environment (chapter 7).

Ecosystems

A group of organisms of the same species in a defined area is called a population. Thus, we might think of a population of gray squirrels in a city park, or a population of robins in a suburban residential neighborhood. The term "community" (or assemblage) is used for two or more populations in a given area. A community of living organisms interacting with its nonliving environment is called an ecosystem.

Ecosystems are essentially self-contained units, with complete food chains (webs) from producers to top predators, that recycle nutrients and other matter and derive energy from the sun to drive the system. Ecosystems may be small, such as a well-balanced pond, or large, such as a wilderness area covering thousands of acres. Natural ecosystems generally are established over many years, are self-sustaining, and exhibit what is frequently called a "balance of nature."

In the truest sense, the term "urban ecosystem" is a misnomer (although it is frequently used) because present-day cities, towns, and villages do not function as ecosystems (as defined in the preceding paragraphs). Unlike natural ecosystems, human-dominated metropolitan areas rely little on solar input as an energy source. Rather, the vast majority of energy (for things such as automobiles and other machines, home and office heating and air-conditioning, and lighting) is derived from coal, oil, and natural gas, and to a lesser extent, nuclear material, from vast areas outside the urban boundary. These energy sources were produced by plants millions of years ago, and we currently are using them up at a rapid rate.

A second major distinction between urban areas and true ecosystems relates to food supply. Considering the most dominant species (humans), food supplies in urban areas are not constrained by food chains within the system. Rather, food is imported from farms and ranches covering vast areas of the rural landscape outside the urban zone.

Third, little recycling of nutrients and other matter occurs in urban areas. Each urban resident in the United States daily uses some 150 gallons (560 liters) of water and generates some 120 gallons (450 liters) of sewage, over 3 pounds (1.3 kilograms) of refuse, and about 1.3 pounds (0.6 kilograms) of air pollutants (Spirn 1984). Practically none of this is recycled within the system, although progress is being made in recycling some of the material outside the urban boundary. As of 1983, about 42% of the sewage sludge generated in the United States was applied to land, 27% was burned, 15% went to landfills, 12% was composted, and 4% was dumped into the ocean (Brown and Jacobson 1987). On a worldwide basis, however, over two-thirds of the nutrients present in human wastes are released to the environment as unreclaimed sewage, often polluting bays, rivers, and lakes (Brown and Jacobson 1987). Closing this nutrient cycle would make ecological sense and would assist efforts to sustain urban systems.

Natural systems are balanced with regard to productivity, consumption, and cycling of matter, and are thus sustainable. It would seem prudent to sustain human society by patterning urban systems along similar lines. The strength of this argument is more easily appreciated when considering human dispersal to space systems beyond the confines of earth. To sustain human populations beyond earth, we need to develop closed, stable, regenerating ecosystems. In reality, the life-support system needed in space is not unlike that required on earth. Many of the problems of human survival in an artificial space system are the same as problems involved in continued survival on earth—the detection and control of air and water pollution, provision of adequate quantities of food of proper nutritional quality, recycling of wastes and garbage, and handling of social problems created by reduced living space. These are all problems that city mayors can easily identify with!

Succession

Vegetational communities change over time within a given area. This process is called succession or biotic change. Succession is a dynamic and continuous process, often occurring gradually over time. For descriptive purposes, changes can be classified into rather distinct stages. For example, during the first year or two on an abandoned farm field in the southeastern United States, annual forbs such as ragweed, horseweed, and crabgrass cover the field. Plants such as goldenrod and asters follow the second and third years. Walking through the field during this early stage of succession, we expect to see and hear such birds as grasshopper sparrows and meadowlarks. The grass-forb stage of succession gradually will be replaced by a grass–shrub–pine-seedling community that will last perhaps 15 to 20 years. Birds such as the yellowthroat and field sparrow will be common. The pine seedlings will continue to grow in the abundant sunlight, and from about year 25 to year 100, a pine forest will dominate the site, providing habitat for birds such as the pine warbler. However, pine seedlings do not grow well in the shade of taller pines, but shade-tolerant oaks and hickories do. In about 150 to 200 years, an oak-hickory forest will replace the pine stand. Birds such as the tufted titmouse, red-eyed vireo, and wood thrush will thrive in the deciduous forest. The seedlings of oak and hickory, capable of growing in the shade of the older trees, will thrive and thus replace the older oaks and hickories that die of disease, old age, or other causes. The oak-hickory community is a climax community. It is capable of replacing itself and continuing until an act of nature, such as fire from lightning, widespread disease outbreak, or human disturbance (for example, logging), sets back succession to an earlier stage. Although this example has been documented for an abandoned farm field (Odum 1971), a similar process would be expected on a vacant urban lot in the region.

Succession progresses from one plant community to another in part because the existing community makes growing conditions more favorable for other plant species. Because different animal communities are dependent on different successional stages, an understanding of succession is of great importance to wildlife biologists. A major component of wildlife management is habitat management.

Urbanization and the associated activities of humans have a profound impact on natural succession, with the result that little natural succession occurs in most metropolitan areas. Reasons for this include the wide use of exotic plant species for landscaping and people's interest in maintaining vast expanses of lawn.

Environmental forces that act on natural plant communities also influence urban communities. Thus, lawns can be maintained only by continuous mowing and application of fertilizers and perhaps other soil amendments, herbicides, and pesticides. Closely cropped grass, however, provides few habitat needs of wildlife. Some use of these areas is made by robins, starlings, and a few other species, but

Retaining as many as possible of the original trees during development minimizes impact on wildlife. Ground vegetation, leaf litter, and the shrub layer also were not removed at this site. (Photo: National Institute for Urban Wildlife.)

wide expanses of closely mown lawn, overall, are detrimental to wildlife.

In urban forested areas, a widespread practice is to clean out the brush understory along with the leaf litter on the forest floor. Frequently, the establishment of shade-tolerant grasses follows this procedure. Loss of the understory and leaf litter is harmful to many wildlife species dependent on these forest features. In the long term, such practice also will lead to loss of the forest itself. As trees die from old age, wind and insect damage, lightning, or other causes, there are no replacements for them because the tree seedlings in the understory have been eliminated. These sites can be replanted at great expense with nursery stock, and there is some value in doing so, but research on birds has shown that no matter how good our intentions, the planted environment does not replace the value of natural forest stands (DeGraaf 1987). Thus, where possible in parks and other open spaces, maintenance of natural forest stands should be encouraged.

Community Change across the Landscape

Broad regions of the earth's land area exhibit characteristic and different types of climax plant communities based largely on climate and soils. These regions may be considered large natural "landscape units" that also support distinct animal communities. For example, grasslands are present on all continents except Antarctica. Characteristic animals of grasslands include grazers such as pronghorn antelope in North America, zebra and wildebeest in Africa, and kangaroos in Australia.

Human influence, through farming, cutting of forests, and urbanization, fragments the natural plant communities into smaller and smaller units. These activities affect not only the plant communities, but the animal communities as well. In North America, farming and ranching have altered the prairies, with major impact on bison, pronghorn antelope, prairie chickens, and other grassland species. The 1860 bison population in the United States has been estimated at 60 million animals, but only 150 bison remained in the wild in 1889 (Robinson and Bolen 1989). Because of establishment of preserves and other measures, the bison has escaped extinction and now exceeds 30,000 animals in North America (Robinson and Bolen 1989). Likewise, prairie chickens once thrived on the grasslands. But today, of the four recognized subspecies, one (eastern heath hen) is extinct, one (Attwater's prairie chicken) is endangered, and populations of greater and lesser prairie chickens are only a fraction of what they once were (Westemeier and Edwards 1987). The pronghorn antelope has fared somewhat better. From an original population estimated at 40 million, fewer than 25,000 pronghorns were present in North America by 1920. Through focused research and sound management practices, however, the present-day population numbers some 1 million animals (Cadieux 1987).

Intensive forestry practices also alter native plant and wildlife communities. For example, short-rotation pine plantations are commonly replacing natural stands of pines and deciduous forests of the southeastern United States. These monotypic stands of closely spaced pines are of less benefit to wildlife than are natural pine stands, and the loss of deciduous woodlands has an even greater impact on a wide variety of animals.

Farming and forestry practices, at first glance, may seem far removed from city life. However, some three-fourths of the North American human population now lives in metropolitan areas, and most of the food produced on farms and ranches goes to urban markets. Likewise, the majority of forest products, such as lumber for houses and other structures and wood pulp for paper and related materials, is consumed by urban residents. So, the influence of urbanization is widespread, indeed.

The process of urbanization also affects natural plant communities in a more direct manner. Baltimore, Maryland, Kansas City, Missouri, and Tucson, Arizona, are located in deciduous forest, grassland, and desert communities, respectively. But with extensive replacement of the ground surface with buildings, roads, parking lots, and other structures, and with the propensity to substitute exotic vegetation for native vegetation, it is sometimes difficult to recognize the natural community types in which cities are located!

The effects of urbanization do not have to be all negative. An understanding of ecological processes and principles, and the will of people to consider the needs of wildlife (as well as a more pleasant environment for society), can lead to minimization of detrimental impacts and, in some instances, to habitat enhancement. Considerable emphasis currently is being placed on landscaping urban and suburban areas with native vegetation. In addition, there are other guidelines for urban development detailed in chapters 6 and 7.

Habitat and Niche

The place where an animal (or plant) resides and finds food, water, cover, and space to grow and reproduce is called habitat. A freshwater marsh, a farm woodlot, and an urban park are habitats for various species of wildlife. With our own continuing demand for more houses, more roads, more energy, and with our advanced technologies and sophisticated machines for meeting those demands, humans place greater and greater pressure on the habitats of other living creatures. The magnitude of these actions has increased in recent human history, but the process of habitat alteration, and its effect on wildlife, has been recognized for a long time, as the following lines reflect:

The law locks up the man or woman,
who steals the goose from the common;
But the greater villain the law lets loose,
who steals the common from the goose.

Anonymous (17th century)

Knowingly or unknowingly, we are all responsible to some degree for "stealing the common from the goose."

The role that an organism plays in an ecosystem is referred to as ecological niche. Cottontail rabbits and red foxes may live in the same habitat, but their roles are different; one is a herbivore, the other a carnivore. Thus, they occupy different niches.

Species in natural ecosystems reduce direct competition with one another by filling specific ecological niches unsuitable (or less suitable) for other species. This relationship, called Gause's principle of competitive exclusion after the noted Russian biologist G. F. Gause ([1934] 1964), is the basis for the much-quoted phrase "one species–one niche." Relationships among the multitude of species in any given ecosystem have developed over many years of coevolution, resulting in a generally stable system referred to earlier as the balance of nature. Different species, sometimes closely related and sometimes unrelated, occupy similar niches in different geographical areas around the world. Such species are called ecological equivalents. For example, kangaroos are herbivores in Australia, filling a niche similar to the one occupied by bison and pronghorn antelope in North America.

Problems often arise when an exotic (nonnative) species is introduced into a habitat containing a native ecological equivalent. Over time, one species—frequently, but not always, the introduced exotic—outcompetes its equivalent, resulting in the demise of the latter. Introduced exotics frequently gain the upper hand because they have not coevolved with the other species in the system, which contains checks and balances on the native species but not on the introduced species. For this reason, populations of introduced species often increase rapidly following arrival in new habitat.

Competition between ecological equivalents frequently relates to food and/or nesting sites. Thus, the exotic house sparrow and starling (introduced into the United States from Europe in 1851 and 1890, respectively) compete for nesting sites with the bluebird, native only to North America. And fierce competitors they are! It is widely believed that the eastern bluebird population is now only about 10% of what it was some 50 years ago. Although there are other factors contributing to the decline of bluebirds (such as widespread use of insecticides and destruction of habitat), competition for nest sites with starlings and house sparrows is considered the major reason for the sharp decline in bluebird numbers (Zeleny 1976). All three species are hole (or cavity) nesters, but starlings and house sparrows are more aggressive birds and successfully outcompete bluebirds for the limited nest sites available in nature.

Humans have stepped into the picture on the side of bluebirds. We now erect and monitor thousands of bluebird boxes (artificial nesting cavities) throughout the United States and Canada. Nesting boxes are constructed to exclude the larger starling (by making the entrance hole too small for the starling to enter), but the smaller house sparrow, about the same size as the bluebird, is more difficult to exclude. Its similar size and aggressive nature make the house sparrow a formidable opponent for the bluebird. Once while monitoring a bluebird trail (a series of bluebird boxes) in Maryland, I found a house sparrow nest with eggs built on top of a bluebird nest containing the dead body of an adult male bluebird, obviously killed defending the nest site. This observation is not uncommon (Zeleny 1976, Gowaty 1984). Without human assistance, surely bluebird populations would continue to decline.

The European mute swan is another exotic species reproducing in the wild in the United States. The species has escaped from captivity in Michigan, New England, and Maryland (Robinson and Bolen 1989). This large, graceful swan is highly regarded in its native homeland. In addition, many urban residents in North America delight in the bird's presence on local lakes and ponds. Because of our knowledge of ecological equivalents and experience with starlings, house sparrows, and other exotic introductions, however, there is some concern among biologists that mute swans in North America may detrimentally impact native waterfowl.

Plants, too, have ecological equivalents around the world. Of particular concern here is people's desire to use exotic species rather than native ones for landscaping around homes, offices, city parks, and other open spaces. As with animals, some exotic plants have escaped to the wild, with detrimental effects on native plants. For example, purple loosestrife, a mainly aquatic plant of Eurasian origin, is now well established and spreading in North America. Its introduction in the United States probably was through a variety of means, including importation from English gardens of the 17th, 18th, and early 19th centuries for use in early American flower gardens (Thompson et al. 1987). The plant offers a striking floral display and its use in garden and border plantings continues in Canada and the United States. Biologists are primarily concerned with purple loosestrife's ability to replace native wetland plant communities with solid stands of loosestrife of little value to wildlife. Because of these and numerous other examples, the introduction of exotic species into new areas should be avoided.

With these ecological factors in mind, let's now focus attention more intensely on the metropolitan landscape–its characteristics, plant and animal communities, and wildlife management possibilities.

Chapter 3

The Metropolitan Setting

For descriptive purposes, it may be helpful to view urban areas as consisting of three zones (VanDruff 1979). The metropolitan center is the densely populated inner-city or downtown area. The ground is covered mostly by buildings, parking lots, and streets, with little room for trees, shrubs, or other vegetation. Because of the bleak habitat, few wildlife species are found, and management opportunities are limited. Nevertheless, with creativity, enhancement may be possible through tree, shrub, and other vegetation plantings along streets and in parking lots, in corner plazas, and even on rooftops and in window gardens. Small, "pocket parks" may be created in redevelopment projects.

Leaving the inner city, one enters a broad zone classified as suburbia. This is the most widespread type of urbanization, and suburbia is less densely developed than the city center. More open space is present here, and wildlife may exist as remnants of former natural communities. Greater management opportunity also is available in suburbia, and naturalistic landscaping can be accomplished for aesthetics and wildlife habitat. In addition, such landscaping can lead to energy cost savings through reduced mowing of grass and other vegetation, and less use of water, fertilizer, and pesticides.

The third zone is the urban-rural interface. Opportunities are available here to preserve from development areas of native habitat such as valuable woodlots and wetlands, thus minimizing impacts on wildlife. With thoughtful planning, development can take place on less valuable sites and the most important wildlife habitat can be saved.

Several characteristics differentiate urban from rural environments. One of the most apparent differences is that urban areas contain many more people. They also have more concrete and asphalt parking lots, streets, and sidewalks and many more buildings than does the rural countryside. Cities, towns, and villages generally have less vegetation (and therefore less shade) and are hotter than rural zones. Metropolitan areas also are dirtier and noisier than the countryside is, and urban streams, lakes, and ponds often are noticeably polluted. Let's examine these characteristics in more detail, particularly their influence on wildlife and habitat.

Human Dominance

Humans, for the most part, are gregarious creatures. In fairly recent history, we have built many magnificent cities to provide living space. And the urbanization process continues, worldwide. The first city to reach a human population of 1 million was probably Beijing or Xian in China around 1800. By 1900, 16 such cities existed, and in 1980 the number increased to some 235. By the year 2025, about 200 megacities will likely exist—each with 4 million to 20 million people (Goode 1991).

In the United States, the human population has increased dramatically since the first census in 1790 (Fig. 2). In its early history, the country was mostly rural based. Since 1940, however, Americans have become increasingly urbanized, to the extent that about 78% of the population now resides in the metropolitan environment (Fig. 3).

The growth rate of the human population in the United States has slowed in recent years (Table 1). In the 1960s and 1970s, growth of the metropolitan population was about twice that of the total population, with people moving to the cities from nonmetropolitan areas. During the 1980s, growth of the metropolitan population was cut almost in half but still remained higher than the total population growth rate, with migration from rural areas continuing. Greatest growth from 1960 to 1988 occurred in cities with populations of 50,000 to 100,000 (U.S. Bureau of the Census 1991). During this time, growth patterns by region differed, with greatest increases occurring in the South and West and negative growth in the Northeast and Midwest (Table 2).

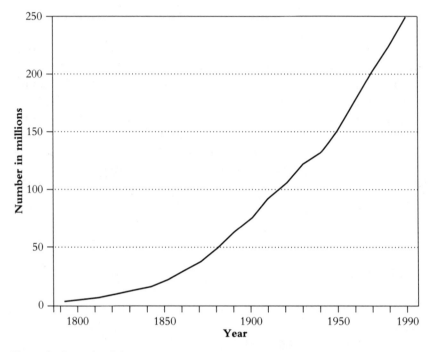

Figure 2. Growth of the U.S. human population, 1790-1990. The expansion places increasing pressure on wildlife as natural habitat is lost to intense human use of the landscape for cities, towns, villages, and agricultural production. (Source: Andriot 1983 and U.S. Bureau of the Census 1991.)

Waterproofed Ground (Surfaces Impervious to Water)

The high percentage of rooftops and concrete and asphalt parking lots, streets, and sidewalks in the urban environment has a major impact on local hydrology. These surfaces "waterproof" the ground surface by creating an impervious barrier to precipitation and thus restrict water infiltration through the soil. Reduced infiltration leads to lower underground water tables and increased surface water runoff (Fig. 4). This surface water runoff is widely described as urban storm-water runoff and may contain polluting sediment and toxic materials in addition to nutrients such as nitrogen and phosphorus washed from lawns, golf courses, and similar areas.

The impact of urban development on streams is particularly noticeable. For example, compared with streams in the countryside, ur-

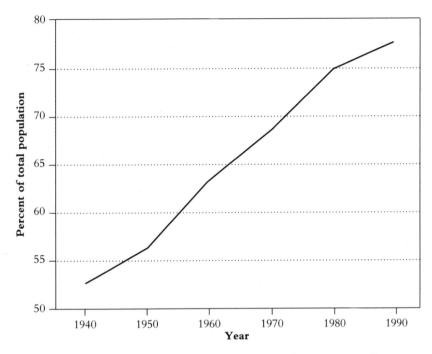

Figure 3. Percentage of the U.S. human population residing in metropolitan areas, 1940-1990. As the population urbanizes, it becomes more difficult for individuals to maintain contact with wildlife and nature. Yet urban residents are interested in these outdoor amenity values, and more effort should be devoted to providing and enhancing such values in the urban landscape. (Source: Robinson and Bolen 1989 and U.S. Bureau of the Census 1991.)

ban streams typically have muddier bottoms with less gravel, and the water is more turbid. One reason for this is that erosion in the surrounding watershed is greater in urban areas. Loss of trees and other vegetation and disturbance of the ground surface at construction sites contribute to increased erosion. Losses of soil from construction sites may range from 30 to 750 tons per acre per year (67-1,680 metric tons per year) (Johnson and Jackson 1980). In contrast, the national average for water erosion on cropland in the United States is some 4.7 tons per acre per year (10.5 metric tons per hectare per year) and even less for forested land (U.S. Department of Agriculture 1981 as cited in Robinson and Bolen 1989). Greater erosion of the stream banks themselves also contributes to turbid, muddy-bottomed

Table 1. Growth rate of the human population in the United States, 1960-1990

Population	Growth rate (%)		
	1960-1970	1970-1980	1980-1990
Metropolitan	23.6	21.5	13.7
Nonmetropolitan	-3.9	-10.5	-2.0
Total	13.4	11.4	9.8

Source: U.S. Bureau of the Census (1991).

Table 2. Movement patterns of the human population in the United States, 1960-1990

Region	Distribution (%)			
	1960	1970	1980	1990
Northeast	24.9	24.1	21.7	20.4
Midwest	28.8	27.8	26.0	24.0
South	30.7	30.9	33.3	34.4
West	15.6	17.1	19.1	21.2
Total	100.0	99.9	100.1	100.0

Source: U.S. Bureau of the Census (1991).

streams in the city, with steep, almost vertical sides. Accelerated erosion of stream banks occurs because the high proportion of impervious ground surface causes a greater quantity of water to move through the channels at high velocity.

To quickly remove this "excess" storm-water runoff, streams may be channelized. This practice was more widespread in the past, but is still used today. It typically involves removing riparian (streamside) overstory vegetation, removing tree branches and logs from the streambed, and straightening the stream channel. At the extreme, channelized urban streams sometimes are modified to flow in concrete channels or, unknown to many people, may be completely out of sight in underground pipes!

A keen observer will note greater variability in stream flows in metropolitan areas. This, too, results from decreased porosity of the ground surface. The simple fact is that less water infiltrates the ground surface to maintain the underground water table. Thus, some streams may dry up completely during summer droughts, and others slow to a trickle. This is devastating to fish and other aquatic organisms.

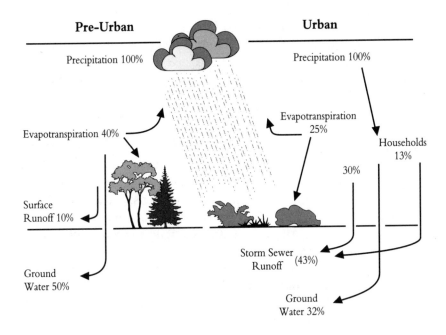

Figure 4. Hydrologic changes caused by urbanization. On undeveloped sites (pre-urban), more precipitation soaks into the ground and less flows overland as surface runoff. Better management of increased surface water runoff after development is needed in most metropolitan areas. (Source: OECD 1986.)

On closer analysis, other differences may separate urban from rural streams. Urban streams usually are warmer than their rural counterparts for several reasons. Streamside vegetation often is removed, sometimes in combination with stream channelization, eliminating the shading effect of trees and shrubs. Precipitation falling on heated streets, parking lots, and rooftops carries added heat to streams. In addition, storm water often is ponded temporarily before being released slowly to a receiving stream. This is done to lessen the impacts of urban runoff, but ponding also warms the water. Management implications of this practice are discussed in more detail in chapter 8.

Urban streams frequently are more heavily polluted than rural ones. Sediment is a major pollutant and causes enormous disturbances to aquatic ecosystems.

Toxic heavy metals such as lead, cadmium, and mercury may be present in elevated levels in metropolitan streams. Many of these metals originate from tire wear and the exhaust of vehicles and from pavement-marking paint. They are washed into streams from roads and streets. Others originate from commercial and industrial developments.

Fertilizers added to urban lawns and other open spaces find their way to local streams and other waters. The yields of nitrogen and phosphorus in runoff may exceed by factors of over 25 and 100 for nitrogen and phosphorus respectively those lower levels considered necessary to limit nuisance algal growths in natural systems (Kim et al. 1978). Pesticide pollution from lawns, gardens, and golf courses is of increasing concern in view of the proliferating application of these chemicals to the soil. All of these impacts tend to reduce the wildlife diversity of urban stream systems.

Perhaps less noticeable than impacts on streams is the impact of urbanization on wetlands generally. This is because wetlands typically have been drained and thus are gone from sight once development is complete. Between the mid-1950s and mid-1970s, annual wetland losses averaged 458,000 acres (185,490 hectares) in the United States (Tiner 1984). Urban development was responsible for some 8% of the losses, and other development accounted for an additional 5%. The remaining 87% resulted from drainage for agricultural use. Although natural wetlands have decreased, constructed lakes and ponds have increased with urban development. These waters do not replace the habitat value of natural streams and wetlands, but they can be enhanced for wildlife (chapter 8).

Altered Climate

One only needs to follow the local weather report to know that temperatures are higher in the city than in the countryside. This and other effects of cities on urban climate are summarized in Table 3.

The increased temperature of cities is a result of human modification of the landscape. Of greatest effect is loss of trees through land clearing and the extensive use of brick, concrete, and asphalt. Loss of trees eliminates their shading effect and results in less surface cooling through evapotranspiration. Thus, cities become so-called urban

Table 3. Some effects of cities on urban climate

Climate element	Compared to countryside
Contaminants	5-25 times more
Sunshine	5%-15% less
Clouds	5%-10% more
Precipitation	5%-15% more
Temperature	1°-6°F (3.3°C) higher
Relative humidity	6% less
Wind speed	20%-30% less

Source: Landsberg (1981) and Herold (1991).

heat islands. The magnitude or intensity of a heat island is measured as the difference between rural and urban temperatures and is positively related to the human population size of the city (Oke 1973). Hot air rises in the center of the city, and cooler air flows in from the surrounding countryside to replace it.

Higher temperature in the city results in a longer growing season for plants and a longer period of ice-free open-water conditions on lakes and ponds. These may influence wildlife use of the habitat.

City air also is dirtier than air in the countryside. Dust, smoke, and exhaust from diesel engines of buses are some readily apparent sources. This matter forms a dust dome over the larger city area, a process that tends to concentrate particulate pollution in the inner city (Bryson and Ross 1972). Dust follows the air currents of the heat island effect and thus tends to move from the edge of the city to the center where it is carried upward with hot air flow. The air cools and dissipates at higher altitudes, and dust settles toward the ground perimeter to repeat the process.

Other less visible pollutants also are present in the urban atmosphere. Oxides of carbon, sulfur, and nitrogen are released into the atmosphere from automobile exhaust and from the burning of fossil fuels in power plants, factories, and refineries. Some chemicals react in the presence of sunlight to produce photochemical smog that hangs as a brownish haze over the city.

Atmospheric pollution interferes with solar radiation. One result is less sunshine over the city near ground level. Such pollution also may be harmful to people as well as to plants and animals of the city.

Smog is irritating to the eyes and respiratory system of humans and is toxic to plants. Effects of atmospheric pollution on plant material was first noticed in the 19th century in the lack of lichens growing in the Luxembourg Garden of Paris (Domrös 1966 as cited in Landsberg 1981). Loss of butterflies in Britain is correlated with atmospheric pollution as indicated by lichen loss and rising sulphur dioxide levels (Barbour 1986).

There are some other less noticeable effects of cities on climate (Bryson and Ross 1972, Landsberg 1981, and Herold 1991). Wind speed is reduced in urban areas largely as a result of the increased surface roughness of various-sized buildings. Some evidence indicates that cities have more clouds and more precipitation than does the surrounding countryside. Unfortunately, the added precipitation is of little use to humans, wildlife, or plants as most of it falls on impermeable surfaces and is quickly lost as urban runoff. Relative humidity is lower in the city because of increased runoff and less vegetation, resulting in reduced evapotranspiration. However, fog frequently is more prevalent in the city because water vapor that is present readily condenses on the more abundant particulate matter. As air is uplifted by convection in the inner city (because of the heat island effect), it cools, promoting water vapor condensation on the accompanying particulate matter and thus cloud formation.

Cities also contribute significantly to the greenhouse effect, ozone depletion, and acid rain. These are global problems, apparent in the countryside as well as in the city, and are beyond the scope of this book.

Increased Noise

Cities are noisy places. Much of the artificial noise generated comes from streets and is associated with transportation (Stevenson 1972). Construction work and industrial operations are other sources of noise, along with air-conditioning units, heat pumps, and garbage trucks.

Until recently, little attention was given to noise. Basically it was assumed that noise was part of the price of industrialized society. But now it is being more seriously considered for a number of reasons. Of greatest concern is hearing loss in humans, resulting from excessive noise. Noise also may be a general annoyance and may interrupt human speech, sleep, and other activities. Noise also has physiological and psychological effects associated with stress and tension although such effects are difficult to quantify.

Human preference for certain sounds is another measure of the importance of the natural world to people. For example, in a recent survey of both city dwellers and country residents (Dawson 1988), "The sound of songbirds pleased the most respondents, with ocean waves a close second, followed by a cat's purr, church bells and wind. . . . Sounds found to be ugly were heavy traffic at rush hour, power saws, sirens, gunfire, dentist's drills, and screams of pain." Dawson concluded that "nature is clearly the leading sound preference, with enjoyable human activity close behind."

Some efforts are now under way to reduce the artificial noise level of the city. Newer airplanes have reduced engine noise, and sound barriers are placed along the rights-of-way of busy streets. Planted shrubs and trees also can be used to lessen noise levels (Reethof and Heisler 1976, Anderson et al. 1984).

The effects of noise on wildlife have not been well studied and are not well understood (Fletcher and Busnel 1978). Some animals seem to habituate to certain noises. For example, I have seen white-tailed deer and wild turkey appear to pay no attention to a busy nearby road with car and truck traffic. Likewise, Canada geese and gulls sometimes use noisy airfields for feeding, nesting, and resting. In some instances, use may become so intense that population control efforts are needed to maintain safe takeoff and landing conditions for aircraft. After exhausting other options, officials at John F. Kennedy International Airport in New York City killed 15,000 gulls that had been using the runway environs during the summer of 1991. At Aberdeen Proving Ground, Maryland, where military ordnance is tested, white-tailed deer and bald eagle populations are thriving and do not appear to be influenced by the noise. Nesting wild turkey hens and hens with broods pay little attention to sonic booms created by aircraft (Lynch and Speake 1978), and the wetlands surrounding the Kennedy Space Center at Cape Canaveral, Florida, support a wide diversity of wildlife. In addition, there are examples of bluebirds nesting successfully in boxes placed along interstate highways. Perhaps noise is less disruptive to open-land species that depend largely on sight and smell for communication rather than on sound.

Noise may be a greater problem, particularly during the breeding season, for quiet-voiced species that depend mainly on sound to attract mates and to establish and maintain territories. It is difficult to imagine how most woodland warblers could communicate near a busy highway. More research is needed on the effects of noise on wildlife.

Chapter 4
Soils and Plant Communities

In chapter 3, I reviewed major characteristics of the urban environment and made brief mention of soils and vegetation. Because of their importance in sustaining wildlife populations, both soils and vegetation are discussed in greater detail in this chapter.

Soils

Soil refers to the thin top layer of sand, silt, and clay on the earth's surface that results from weathering of bedrock. Some soils weather in place, whereas others form in one location but are transported and deposited elsewhere. River deltas, flood plains, and many valley floors have soils formed from upstream water erosion. Soil particles may be transported a considerable distance before being deposited in the new location. Other soils and soil-forming material may be moved by ice, wind, or gravity.

Soils are highly variable in their physical and chemical makeup. They are defined and classified by the proportions of sand, silt, and clay that they contain. A sandy soil generally will be dry and light because such soil does not hold moisture very well. A clay soil may be wet and heavy from recent rains or dry and almost rock hard if drought conditions prevail. Different percentages of sand, silt, and clay result in various loam soils.

Most plants grow in soil, from which they derive moisture, nutrients, and a foundation for growth. Thus, soils are extremely important in supporting the variety of vegetation communities on earth, and the various vegetation communities are vital for sustaining diverse wildlife populations.

Urban soils generally are much different from soils in the surrounding countryside. Excavation, filling, and grading for buildings, roads, and other structures and facilities greatly disturb the soil. Frequently, the productive topsoil layer is removed and never replaced. In other situations, the topsoil is mixed with subsoil during excavation or other earth-moving activities, and no effort is made to replace the rich top layer in final regrading of the site.

Urban soils often are highly compacted and poorly drained and aerated, with limited or confined rooting space (Craul 1985). Interrupted nutrient cycling also is a major problem as a result of loss of organic matter as leaves and other organic material are "cleaned up" and removed. Compaction may result from repeated human foot traffic or from heavy construction equipment as well as automobiles and other vehicles. Compaction reduces pore space between soil particles; pore space ideally should make up about 50% of the volume of the soil. Adequate oxygen in the soil is necessary for plant growth and should be about 20% of the volume of the soil, with carbon dioxide levels less than 1%. In compacted soils, oxygen may drop to 1% and carbon dioxide rise to 19%, in which case the soil can change from an aerobic (containing oxygen) to an anaerobic (lacking oxygen) condition. When this occurs, soil microorganisms needed to maintain fertility are killed, and it is difficult to reestablish aerobic conditions. Stockpiling of topsoil for extended periods of time for respreading following development also kills soil microbes.

Soil compaction creates resistance to root penetration and increases surface runoff and erosion. To alleviate soil compaction, it may be necessary to restrict human access in certain areas. Alternatively, good results may be obtained by tilling in lightweight aggregates such as "expanded slate," a commercially available material with high porosity. Leaves and other naturally produced organic matter also should be included as soil amendments.

In redevelopment projects, broken brick, mortar, concrete, asphalt, and other debris may be mixed with the soil, further reducing its capability of supporting plant life. A widespread problem with such soils is lack of available nitrogen. Research in Britain indicates that the most effective way of building up soil nitrogen is by use of legumes, especially white clover, which can rapidly accumulate nitrogen in a mineralizable form in the soil (Bradshaw 1982). Legumes help to build up nutrients to levels allowing adequate cycling, whereas artificial fertilizer is not effective in building soil nutrients (Bloomfield et al. 1982).

Plant Communities

Perhaps because of the ubiquitous nature of plants, we tend to ignore their true value in the landscape. However, in addition to their role as primary producers in food chains, plants provide cover and space for wildlife. This is why vegetation management is so important to wildlife management.

Plants also help to maintain proper water balance within ecosystems and to control soil erosion. Above-ground leaves and stems break the impact of raindrops, and extensive underground root systems help to hold soil in place. Much of the precipitation falling on natural communities thus soaks into the ground, providing moisture for growing plants and also maintaining underground water tables. The evapotranspiration process, by cycling moisture back into the atmosphere, aids in cloud formation and more rain.

Trees, shrubs, and other vegetation help to control air and water pollution. As much as 75% of the coarse fraction of dust is removed from urban air moving across parks with trees and shrubs (Landsberg 1981). Through photosynthesis, carbon dioxide is removed from the atmosphere. This function is becoming increasingly recognized and appreciated as concern heightens about global warming. Carbon dioxide is one of several so-called greenhouse gasses that trap the infrared heat from the earth's surface as it is radiated back toward space, and certain human activities, such as the burning of fossil fuels, release carbon dioxide to the atmosphere. Increasing the number of trees through active planting programs is one way of reversing the buildup of atmospheric carbon dioxide. During the growth process, atmospheric carbon is incorporated into the woody structure of stems and branches where it remains until the wood decomposes or is burned. Trees and other vegetation also act as buffers along streams and other waterways, soaking up nutrients washing from urban and agricultural areas that might otherwise pollute these waters. Soil erosion also is reduced with use of such buffers.

Trees and other plants in urban open spaces provide multiple benefits to society. Surveys show that people consider wildlife to be an important component of such areas. (Photo: National Institute for Urban Wildlife.)

In addition to these "ecosystem" values, plants have aesthetic appeal to humans and are useful in landscape architecture. Trees, shrubs, and other vegetation also help to muffle the noise of busy streets and highways, and they lessen the impact of the heat island effect discussed in chapter 3. Deciduous trees may block 90% of the sunlight during summer months (Youngberg 1983). In urban areas, particularly, these are welcome attributes. Even so, many such areas are lacking in vegetation and could realize more pleasant surroundings and energy savings with the planting of more trees and other vegetation. An additional 25% increase in urban tree cover could save 40% or more of the annual cooling energy use of an average house in Sacramento, California, and 25% or more in Phoenix, Arizona, and Lake Charles, Louisiana (Huang et al. 1987).

Plants also have utilitarian value in medicine, agriculture, and industry. Some 25% of all prescriptions dispensed from community pharmacies in the United States contain active ingredients that are extracted from higher plants (Farnsworth and Morris 1976 as cited in

Table 4. Loss of native plant species with increasing urbanization in Poland

Type of settlement	Native species present (%)
Forest settlements	70-80
Small towns	60-65
Medium towns	50-60
Cities	30-50

Source: Falinski (1971) as cited in Kowarik (1990).

Farnsworth 1988). Similar arguments can be made for plants in agriculture and industry.

Considerable potential exists in metropolitan areas for growing trees, shrubs, and other vegetation. In fact, in temperate regions of the world, 60% to 80% of a city's area supports enough trees to meet conventional definitions of "forest" (Rowntree 1984a). However, natural plant communities typically are heavily modified by urbanization. Much vegetation is eradicated and replaced with pavement and buildings, leaving less growing space for plants. Composition and structure of the vegetation also are altered. As urbanization intensifies, native vegetation is replaced by exotic species (Table 4). In what was formerly West Berlin, Germany, some 41% of 1,432 plant species are now nonnative (Kowarik 1990). Many species that were abundant in 1864 were rare by 1987. Some 58% of native species are now endangered, compared with 37% of the so-called archeophytes (exotic plants introduced before 1500 A.D.) and 12% of the neophytes (aliens introduced after 1500 A.D.). Over 230 of the neophytes are more abundant today than in 1864.

A similar pattern exists in the United States. For example, five major plant community types were recorded throughout the metropolitan areas of Akron, Cleveland, Canton, and Youngstown, Ohio, and these became increasingly modified toward urban centers (Whitney and Adams 1980). An "old oak" forest community was found on large residential lots at the urban-rural fringe of all the cities. It most resembled the original mixed oak forest and mixed mesophytic forest of northeastern Ohio and contained an understory of native dogwood and sassafras, with introduced species (eastern hemlock, Japanese maple, and yew) near the homes. Also near the perimeter of the cities was a mixed suburban complex, a diverse plant community with a highly manicured, landscaped appearance. Representative species largely confined to the complex were American holly, tulip poplar, and sweetgum. Continuing toward the city center, three other plant community types were noted — a maple, a conifer, and an inner-city complex. All three generally had a low density of trees and few landscape plantings. Norway maple and silver maple dominated the maple complex; eastern arborvitae and Colorado blue spruce were major conifers; and tree of heaven, Norway maple, and white mulberry were major inner-city trees. The latter species (all aliens) are noted for tolerating stress conditions.

Vegetation structure usually is simplified by urbanization. Often, the ground leaf layer in wooded areas is removed and replaced with shade-tolerant grass. This practice disrupts the breakdown and decay of the leaf litter into rich organic matter that helps to build soils. Likewise, the shrub layer often is removed or heavily modified, creating a savanna-type community (Dorney et al. 1984). Such actions are devastating to the wood thrush and other birds that depend on the forest floor and the shrub layer for food and nest sites.

Closely related factors that positively influence bird use of urban habitats include the number of tree species, tree density, the presence of both deciduous and coniferous species, and nearness to a woodlot. These factors largely explain why more species of birds use suburban residential lots than use more heavily developed urban lots (DeGraaf and Wentworth 1981). Urban lots lacking natural stands of forest and secure open nesting habitat will not support insectivorous or ground-nesting birds. Populations of many of these birds are declining, and stronger conservation measures are needed.

As areas undergo urbanization, a recognizable pattern emerges, reflecting three broadly defined plant community categories. First, there usually are some remnants of natural communities that remain after development. These make up a small component of the urban vegetation complex and often lose some of their natural qualities over time. For example, four natural forest stands were retained on the York University campus in Toronto, Ontario. However, 30% of the vascular species have been lost since 1968. The rapid decline in plant diversity, structure, and composition is attributed primarily to drastic changes in hydrology and to an evolving urban climate brought on by increasing campus development (Boyer et al. 1986). One result has been the transformation of a sustained and balanced moisture regime into one of extremes—spring flooding and summer drought.

Frequently, exotic plants from surrounding development invade urban natural areas and, over time, displace many of the native species. Thus, common dandelion and orange hawkweed (both aliens) from an adjacent residential development were found along the edge and 98 feet (30 meters) within a sugar maple forest in central New York (Moran 1984). In another instance, of the 343 plant species recorded in Van Cortlandt Park, a 1,132-acre (458-hectare) New York City park, 28% were not native (Profous and Loeb 1984).

Urbanization has similar effects on natural plant communities in the aquatic environment. Storm-water runoff pollutes nearby streams with constituents from soil fertilizers and other soil amendments. Thus, streams draining residential and agricultural areas in the New Jersey Pine Barrens had higher pH values and nitrogen levels than did nearby unpolluted streams (Morgan and Philipp 1986). The primary effect of pollution was replacement of a distinctive Pine Barrens flora with one containing many marginal or nonindigenous species common to wetlands throughout the eastern United States.

In addition to remnant natural communities, a second urban plant community category encompasses those plants that make up colonizing communities that are found on vacant lots and waste or derelict lands. Little study of plant ecology of such sites has occurred in North America. More work has been done in England and Europe, and some patterns revealed there probably have application to North America as well. Vegetation of such sites is dominated by aliens. Species found typically have wide geographical and ecological ranges, and they tend to be species of early successional stages, with rapid growth and dispersal rates. They have evolved a strategy to rapidly disperse and fill available niches, following land disturbance, and often are referred to as "pioneer" species. Such species usually are common or abundant on recently disturbed urban sites (Hodgson 1986).

A third recognizable category of urban plant communities, and by far the largest, is what might be termed "planted communities." This component includes public and private open spaces of parks, institutional grounds, and businesses, as well as street rights-of-way and residential backyards. Unlike the other two components, planted communities are characterized by active human effort to plant various trees, shrubs, and other vegetation. Such landscaping is mostly practiced in high-use public areas, near buildings, along streets, and in individual yards, although business parks and other campus settings may have rather extensive grounds of landscaping. Some original trees and shrubs may be retained during development but overall the category consists mostly of new plantings.

The types of plants used in landscaping depend on several factors. Critically important is the economic well-being of individuals, businesses, industries, and cities, because if little or no money is available, little or no landscaping will occur. In addition, planting stock must be available, adapted to the area, and capable of growing under stressful conditions. In the southwest United States for example, drought-hardy trees and shrubs are needed. Among the plants recommended for urban revegetation and landscaping under such conditions are red buckeye, canyon maple, Lacey oak, osage-orange, and evergreen sumac (Dewers 1981).

Another factor that is important in determining the types of plants used in landscaping is changing patterns of landscape taste and fashion. Historically, landscaping in North America has tended to follow the English tradition of intensively managed and tidy formal plantings of mostly exotic species and close-mown grass. Since the 1970s, however, increasing interest has been shown in more natural landscaping, pioneered by the Dutch in the Netherlands. Since the late 1960s, Dutch "ecological landscapes" have represented a new approach to the design of urban open space (Ruff 1987). Ecological processes such as plant succession and concepts such as the linking of diversity and stability are adopted as bases of design. Emphasis also is placed on use of native species. The result is a less formal and more natural appearance. Such ecological landscapes integrate passive and active recreation, serve environmental education functions, and better assist in the conservation of plants and wildlife. This trend seems to be gaining more acceptance in North America although it certainly has not replaced formal landscaping.

The most widespread, formal tree-planting program of municipalities involves "street trees." Such trees are planted primarily for shade and aesthetics, with little thought given to their value to wildlife. Further, cities have relied on a very narrow range of species for their planting programs. More than 90% of all street trees planted during the 1970s in 23 municipalities in southern Ontario were Norway maple, linden, ash, mountain ash, crab apple, and honey locust

(Pickering and Perkins 1982). In Syracuse, New York, Norway maple, silver maple, and sugar maple constitute two-thirds of the street trees (Rowntree and Sanders 1981).

Relying on only a few tree species greatly increases the potential for total tree loss from insects or disease. The reason for this is that plant insects and diseases are generally quite host specific, and if a given host is widespread and abundant, then almost unlimited growth of a particular insect population or disease organism can occur. This can be devastating to the host plant. For example, many developing municipalities in the United States planted American elms along streets. This is a magnificent tree well suited for such a role. The accidental import of Dutch elm disease earlier in the 20th century, however, is methodically killing city elms, and many municipalities that relied on this species are losing entire tree populations. The disease is spread by elm bark beetles. Urban elms are especially hard hit because such trees typically occur as monoculture plantings. Once the disease appears, it spreads rapidly because of the ease with which bark beetles can move from tree to tree. This is one of the hazards of relying on single species monocultures, or of relying on only a few species of plants. If community planners maintain more diversity in street tree–planting programs, insect or disease attack on any one species will not likely destroy the entire tree community. Greater plant diversity also results in greater wildlife diversity.

Street trees are exposed to tremendous environmental stresses including water and heat stress, air pollutants such as ozone, sulfur dioxide, and nitrogen oxides, road and street deicing salts, physical barriers to root growth, poor soil quality, reduced sunlight, and damage by vehicles. Little wonder that it is difficult to get them to grow!

With these factors in mind, several recommendations can be made for enhancing street tree growth and survival (Bassuk and Whitlow 1987). First, one can select trees that are relatively tolerant of stressful conditions. Good salt tolerance has been shown by serviceberry, Russian olive, rugosa rose, eastern red cedar, white oak, and red oak (Dirr 1976, 1978). These also are good wildlife plants. On the other hand, good wildlife plants greatly injured by salt include white pine, American beech, eastern hemlock, and autumn olive. Plants show differences with regard to tolerance to other pollutants, too (Table 5).

Table 5. Tree tolerance to sulfur dioxide and ozone

Tolerant	Sensitive
White fir	Common serviceberry
Sugar maple	Red ash
Western juniper	Jack pine
Blue spruce	Quaking aspen
Red oak	
Northern white cedar	
Basswood	

Source: Davis and Gerhold (1976).

Fourteen years after being planted along streets in Philadelphia, Pennsylvania, Kwanzan oriental cherry, black locust, Chinese elm, Japanese pagoda tree, ginkgo, and English oak were the most successful of 15 species rated in terms of growth rates and freedom from insects and disease (Rhoads et al. 1981).

Street tree growth and survival also might be enhanced by changing the way in which trees are planted along city streets (Bassuk and Whitlow 1987). Where possible, providing larger and better-drained pits for individual trees surrounded by concrete or asphalt will help, although maintaining a continuous horizontal soil column between pits would be even better. Use of porous pavement would allow more water to filter into the ground, thus helping to maintain soil moisture. Grouping of plantings in slightly raised beds would have several advantages. Raised beds would act as barriers to salt water runoff in northern cities and towns where slippery winter streets are deiced with salt, and group plantings would have greater aesthetic impact and provide substantial shade. In addition, maximizing the amount of clumped vegetation is a recommended enhancement feature for birds (DeGraaf 1987) and benefits other wildlife as well.

Another major component of the urban planted community is the residential yard. One recent study found that one- and two-family residential lots covering 46% of the land area represented the dominant land-use class in Birmingham, Alabama, Cincinnati and Dayton, Ohio, and Syracuse, New York (Rowntree 1984b). Thus, this component may well be the largest planted community component in the urban environment.

Plant communities of residential lots are highly variable and based on individual owner's tastes. However, many homeowners are enhancing their yards for wildlife by selecting plant material with wildlife considerations in mind. Readers interested in such activity may find appendices A and B helpful.

In terms of ecological productivity, lawns are equivalent to other managed grasses such as corn and wheat (Falk 1980). However, unlike these food products, little use is made of lawn primary productivity in the energy pyramid. Most of the production (lawn clippings) is discarded in curbside trash bags on a weekly basis during the growing season.

In summary, the characteristics of urban soils and plant communities greatly influence wildlife. Almost always, with increasing urbanization of natural habitats, species diversity of plants and animals declines, but density of a few species increases. These relationships are discussed in greater detail in chapter 5.

Chapter 5

Animal Populations and Communities

In chapter 1, I mentioned a variety of examples of wildlife diversity in various urban habitats. Here, I will focus more closely on wildlife populations and communities. A population is a group of organisms of the same species, occupying a certain area during a specific time. We might be interested in the population of gray squirrels in Lafayette Park, adjacent to the White House in Washington, D.C., or the population of Inca doves in Tucson, Arizona. Two or more populations in a given area constitute a community, and we may think in terms of plant communities as well as animal communities. In considering both plants and animals, biologists refer to the biotic community. The biotic community and the nonliving components of the environment make up ecosystems.

To begin our discussion, let's examine characteristics of populations that individual animals do not possess. Most species have a tremendous potential for increase. For example, a pair of bobwhite quail (a very small population) may increase from two to 14 over the course of a single breeding season, representing a 700% increase in the population. A pair of cottontails may increase from two to 24, a 1,200% increase! Thus, a population exhibits a birth rate (natality) that might be expressed as the number of births per 100 individuals per year, or that might be described in relation to some other unit of the population.

In nature, populations show a "normal" rate of increase that is always less than the potential because of environmental limitations, or limiting factors. Natural limiting factors include availability of food, water, and cover, or predation, disease, and territorial requirements of species. Limiting factors influence the death rate (mortality) of a population. Thus, the normal rate of increase for bobwhite quail would more typically be about 250% (instead of 700%) from spring to fall and for cottontails 200% to 500% (rather than 1,200%).

In urban and other human-modified environments, limiting factors may include toxic substances, automobiles, pets (particularly cats and dogs), overhead wires, towers, and windows. Even with these additional impacts, it is generally the absence of adequate habitat components (food, water, cover, and space) in urban areas that is most limiting.

Populations are said to be "stable" when the annual rate of increase is equal to the rate of loss. In addition to natality and mortality, another factor affecting population stability is animal movement. New animals may move into (immigrate), and some animals may leave (emigrate), the population. Young animals, particularly, disperse from the home ranges of their parents in the fall.

Under natural conditions, populations exhibit a characteristic density, or number of individuals per acre or some other unit of area. Density is dependent on the carrying capacity of the land, and factors that determine carrying capacity are limiting factors.

A population will have an age structure that simply reflects the distribution of numbers of individuals of various ages. The proportion of individuals of breeding age influences the birth rate, and the proportion of old animals influences the death rate. Any given population also will exhibit a sex ratio that affects reproductive potential. Populations have a number of other characteristics, but these are beyond the scope of this book.

The remainder of this chapter will consider how wildlife populations thrive or fail in various urban habitats; how urbanization affects populations, communities, and individual species; and some of the adaptive characteristics of animals that allow exploitation of such areas.

Birds

Although our knowledge of bird communities in urban areas is still incomplete, some patterns are emerging. We know that the ur-

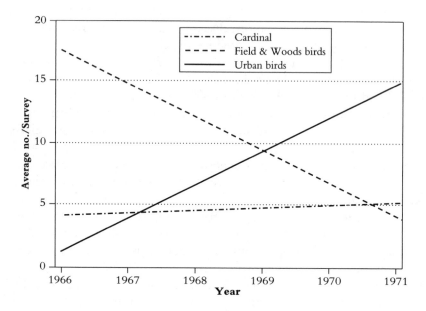

Figure 5. Changes in breeding bird populations during early development of Columbia, Maryland, based on data of Geis (1974). Species composition changes with urbanization as habitat conditions change. (Source: Adams and Dove 1989.)

ban development process fragments the natural landscape. In so doing, it destroys habitat required for many species, modifies habitat of others, and creates new habitat for some species (Fig. 5). Natural vegetation destroyed in the development process generally impacts birds classified as habitat specialists most severely. These are birds that require woodland, for example, flycatchers, vireos, and many of the warblers. They cannot live in downtown centers, open habitats consisting of lawns and shrubs, or even scattered trees characteristic of most suburban areas. As a group, these birds tend to be long-distance migrants and insectivorous in feeding habits.

Modified habitat and newly created habitat, both of which are likely in the wake of urbanization, are most attractive to birds called habitat generalists—birds capable of using a wider range of habitat types. Birds in this category include the mockingbird, song sparrow, chipping sparrow, house wren, mourning dove, catbird, and others. Most of these birds are edge species—they typically live where two

Table 6. Some differences in bird communities of urban habitats compared with natural habitats

Community attribute	Urban habitat	Natural habitat
Abundance of exotic species	High	Low
Abundance of native species	Low	High
Number of species	Low	High
Biomass	High	Low
Density	High	Low
Method of feeding	Generalists: many are seed eaters or feed on a variety of plants and animals.	Specialists: many are primarily insect eaters.

Source: Compiled from many studies, including Emlen (1974), Walcott (1974), Gavareski (1976), Lancaster and Rees (1979), Aldrich and Coffin (1980), Beissinger and Osborne (1982), Penland (1984), and Mills et al. (1989).

or more habitat types meet (for example, where woodland joins open meadow or where woodland fringe joins suburban lawn). As a group, these birds tend to be short-distance migrants or permanent residents (nonmigratory) and granivorous (seed eating) or omnivorous.

As development intensifies, the number of native species of birds declines and more exotic species appear in the community (Table 6). In fact, the most common birds typically found associated with metropolitan centers in the United States are house sparrows, pigeons (also called rock doves), and starlings. All three species are exotics, having been introduced to North America in the early 1700s (pigeon), 1850 (house sparrow), and 1890 (starling). These birds may make up 80% of the city bird community during summer months and some 95% of the community during winter (Johnsen and Van-Druff 1987).

Why these species are so successful in urban environments is not fully understood, but all have a long association with humans in Europe and undoubtedly have strengthened their adaptive characteristics through evolution. These birds make use of an abundant and readily available food supply directly or indirectly from humans. Rural house sparrows have been noted feeding mostly on cereal grains (particularly corn) and insects, whereas urban birds feed heavily on bird seed at feeders, grains and other seeds, and insects (Gavett and Wakeley 1986).

Starlings and pigeons living in the city may feed both there and in the surrounding countryside (Levesque and McNeil 1986, Peach and Fowler 1989). Most probably, if food is plentiful, movement is restricted.

In addition to exploiting a readily available and abundant food supply, urban house sparrows, pigeons, and starlings make use of numerous nesting sites created by humans. Sparrows and starlings nest in house ventilation louvers and other nooks and crannies of modern architecture. Populations are higher in neighborhoods where such nest sites are plentiful (Geis 1976). House sparrows and starlings are aggressive birds, and commonly outcompete other species for nesting sites and food. In chapter 2, I reviewed the impact of these two species on bluebirds, another cavity-nesting species. In addition, starlings can successfully take over nest cavities of many other birds, including, in North America, woodpeckers, purple martins, wood ducks, and buffleheads (Kerpez and Smith 1990).

Pigeons are attracted to open ledges, particularly those with overhanging cover, although birds have been found recently to also nest in enclosed holes or open cavities in tall trees in the city (Peterson 1986). The roof support structures of open amphitheaters provide dry, secure nesting and roosting sites, much to the dismay of human theatergoers trying to enjoy an outdoor concert! By building cities for their own occupation, humans have unwittingly provided ideal conditions for these birds as well. In some instances, we are so successful in providing good habitat that control of populations is needed.

The loss of native habitat specialists as urban development intensifies results from a reduction in natural plant communities. Native trees, shrubs, and ground vegetation are removed or greatly reduced, and native birds have coevolved with such natural plants and are dependent on them for survival. In northern Virginia, researchers compared breeding-bird use of a mature eastern deciduous forest in 1942 with bird use of the same area in 1979, after it had become a well-established residential community (Aldrich and Coffin 1980). Typical forest birds present in 1942, but absent or lacking in 1979, included wood thrushes, red-eyed vireos, ovenbirds, and scarlet tanagers. However, gray catbirds, American robins, and house spar-

Intensive human use of the landscape for agricultural production and housing and other development fragments natural habitats. Many forest wildlife species cannot survive in small, isolated woodlots. (Photo: National Institute for Urban Wildlife.)

rows were numerous in 1979, but were absent from the area in 1942. These researchers concluded that *"if we want both groups of species we must make certain that sufficiently large and undisturbed areas of the natural habitats are preserved to support the breeding of those specialized species that are dependent upon them"* (emphasis added).

Likewise, in Arizona, loss of native vegetation accompanying increased urbanization has altered the bird community, with the disappearance of some species and the addition of others. Black-tailed gnatcatchers, pyrrhuloxias, brown towhees, and black-throated sparrows are the most sensitive to vegetation changes. These species are typically found in surrounding desert but apparently cannot adapt to exotic vegetation or the increased density of buildings in Tucson. Inca doves and house sparrows are the most abundant species in the city (Tweit and Tweit 1986).

Because of favorable nesting sites and abundant food for some species (and perhaps other factors, such as warmer microclimate), the total bird biomass (or weight) and density of birds may well be higher in urban areas compared with surrounding natural habitat. Researchers in Ohio found that the biomass of birds living in a residential area of the city of Oxford was over 2.7 times the biomass of birds found in a nearby natural forest and that the density of birds was more than 1.3 times greater in Oxford (Beissinger and Osborne 1982). A similar, but more pronounced, pattern has been observed in Arizona where one researcher reported that both biomass and density were 26 times greater in the city of Tucson than in the surrounding desert (Emlen 1974). A greater quantity of water used in the city (particularly for watering lawns) may be largely responsible for this difference.

Waterfowl and Other Waterbirds

Various bodies of water in the urban environment may support a diversity of waterfowl and other waterbirds, particularly if such areas are actively managed. Tinicum Marsh, near Philadelphia, Pennsylvania, is a good example of a natural area preserved in the face of encroaching development. The marsh is managed by the U.S. Fish and Wildlife Service as a national wildlife refuge and provides habitat for a variety of wildlife. More than 280 bird species have been recorded there (Anonymous 1989). Unlike Tinicum, however, most water habitats in cities and suburbs consist of constructed lakes, storm-water control and other impoundments, and sewage lagoons. In North America, two birds—the mallard and the Canada goose—are frequently the most common waterfowl inhabitants of such areas.

The mallard is the most common duck in North America and inhabits cities throughout the Northern Hemisphere (Bellrose 1976, Figley and VanDruff 1982). The density of birds may be high in urban areas. Three factors are important in this regard. First, the mallard is highly adaptable and readily adjusts to the urban environment. This characteristic is not found in the black duck, a close relative that requires more secluded habitat. Second, warmer temperatures in the urban environment result in more ice-free water during winter. During hard winters when natural waters are frozen, mallards move to cities and towns for food and open water (Hansson 1966 and Gyllin and Larsson 1967 as reported in Figley and VanDruff 1982). The mallard population is expanding eastward in the United States from the

Midwestern and central states and is quite common in urban–suburban areas. Park mallards in Massachusetts began developing in the late 1930s, and by the early 1980s more than 16,000 waterfowl (mostly mallards) were wintering in the state in park and parklike situations (Heusmann and Burrell 1984). In Massachusetts, virtually all wintering by mallards occurs in parks (Heusmann 1981). Third, and perhaps most important, supplemental feeding by humans is a major factor contributing to maintenance of high densities (Figley and VanDruff 1982, Heusmann and Burrell 1984).

Although the density of mallards may be high in urban areas, little is known about nest success and bird survival in such areas. We do know that the birds typically start to nest four to six weeks earlier in urban areas and also nest later in the fall, perhaps because of warmer conditions in the city and abundant food. The birds also will nest in a variety of locations, even under ornamental shrubbery next to house foundations, woodpiles, and boats (Figley and VanDruff 1982, Master and Oplinger 1984). In Columbia, Maryland, I am aware of mallard hens occasionally nesting successfully in a second-floor, outdoor patio of a downtown office building. The site provides protection against terrestrial mammalian predators such as skunks, raccoons, foxes, and dogs, but hatched ducklings, unable to fly, have no way down to the ground and open water other than with human assistance down the staircase or elevator!

In most instances, brood survival in the city is probably low. Mortality of ducklings from hatching to fledging may be 60% to 70% or higher (Figley and VanDruff 1982, Master and Oplinger 1984). In more natural settings, brood survival is higher as a result of better feeding and escape cover and absence of artificial hazards found in the urban environment. Reproductive success in the city may be high, however, because of renesting opportunities that may more than compensate for low survival of young.

Urban mallard populations differ from natural populations in another respect. Under natural conditions, the mallard has the most balanced sex ratio of all common ducks. The percentage of males during the breeding season is approximately 52% (Bellrose 1976). In urban areas, however, survival of drakes is commonly higher than survival of hens, resulting in sex ratios unnaturally weighted in favor of drakes (Heusmann 1981). In Columbia, Maryland, I have observed populations containing 65% drakes. Groups of two or more excess males frequently harass hens, including those with broods, and repeated rapes or rape attempts occur, occasionally resulting in drownings of hens (which distorts the sex ratio even more). Broods often become scattered and may not reassemble. Lone ducklings are seen, and probably sustain high mortality. Hens in these dense populations are less attentive to broods, a behavior that probably also contributes to higher mortality of ducklings.

Domestic ducks frequently are released on urban impoundments by people who raised the birds from ducklings but will no longer care for them. Mallards readily mate with such birds, resulting in hybrids variously colored and typically heavy bodied. Hybrids may have difficulty flying, and the mixing of gene pools reduces the integrity of the wild mallard pool. Perhaps of more concern is the increased potential for disease transmission from domestic birds to wild waterfowl. One such disease, duck virus enteritis (DVE), also called duck plague, is of particular concern to biologists. DVE is caused by a herpesvirus (not transferable to humans) and was not recorded in North America until 1967 when an outbreak occurred in the white Pekin duck industry on Long Island, New York. Most subsequent outbreaks have involved commercial, avicultural, captive-raised, or city park–type waterfowl. One important exception was a major outbreak in migratory waterfowl in January 1973 at Lake Andes National Wildlife Refuge, South Dakota, where more than 40,000 mallards and lesser numbers of Canada geese and other species died (Brand 1987).

The Canada goose is now frequently a common sight in urban areas throughout North America. Geese were extirpated by hunting and habitat loss over much of their southern breeding range during European settlement. In restoration efforts, many birds were live-captured and relocated to establish other populations.

Releases in urban–suburban areas began in the 1950s, and a decade later geese were breeding in Denver, Colorado, Minneapolis–St. Paul, Minnesota, Detroit, Michigan, Toronto, Ontario, Wilmington, Delaware, suburbs of Boston, Massachusetts, and several communities in New York, New Jersey, and Connecticut (Hawkins 1970). Some of these urban populations have grown rapidly. In 1968, the Minneapolis–St. Paul population was estimated to be about 450 birds (Hawkins 1970). By 1986, it totaled some 10,000 to 12,000 birds (Cooper 1987). Warmer urban temperatures and supplemental

Urban populations of Canada geese are thriving in many municipalities throughout North America. Lakes and ponds and lawns for grazing are key habitat features attractive to the birds. Such populations require management. (Photo: Jay Anderson.)

feeding by humans, along with hunting restrictions, are influential factors in the growth of such populations. The numerous lakes and reservoirs and surrounding open land for grazing (such as lawns, golf courses, and parks) also are attractive to the birds, and islands provide good nest sites and keep predation low. In addition, young geese typically return to nest where they learned to fly.

In contrast to urban mallard ducklings, urban goslings show a survival rate that typically is high and compares well with that of wild populations (Master and Oplinger 1984). Several factors contribute to high survival of young. Both parents strongly protect their brood, orphaned young are readily accepted by other parents, and the birds have low sensitivity to crowding.

Mallards, geese, and a variety of marsh birds and shorebirds make use of urban impoundments constructed for storm-water control. If greater consideration is given to wildlife, the value of such areas can be enhanced. In Columbia, Maryland, two colleagues and I found that use of shallow ponds (ponds with an interspersion of wetland

Even small ponds in the midst of the city provide habitat to some species of wildlife. This one is adjacent to the Department of the Interior building in Washington, D.C. (Photo: National Institute for Urban Wildlife.)

vegetation closely resembling that in freshwater marshes) by breeding pairs of mallards is about 2.4 times greater than use of deep ponds (ponds with mostly open water and steep sides), and about 3.2 times greater than use of lakes (Adams et al. 1985a). Hens with broods of ducklings also preferred shallow ponds to deep ponds and lakes. The same general use pattern is noted for a variety of other wetland birds, including great blue heron, green-backed heron, killdeer, common snipe, yellowlegs, red-winged blackbirds, and spotted, solitary, and least sandpipers (Adams et al. 1985b).

Larger reservoirs and lakes may be constructed in urban areas for storm-water control also, but generally these will be designed primarily for recreation. They are not as valuable for wildlife during the breeding season as are the smaller impoundments. During migration and winter, however, most waterfowl species flock and tend to use the larger bodies of water as roosts to avoid disturbance. In the northeastern and mid–Atlantic regions, a variety of waterfowl species use these larger impoundments during migration and over winter as resting and feeding sites (Figley and VanDruff 1982, Master and Oplinger 1984, Adams et al. 1986). These commonly include Canada geese, blue-winged teal, ring-necked ducks, canvasbacks, and lesser scaup.

Another type of human-created habitat for waterfowl and other waterbirds in urban areas is the sewage lagoon. Such facilities are common near most metropolitan areas. Although they are designed for treating human sanitary waste, they also are noted by bird-watchers as "hot" birding spots. Birds are attracted mainly to the areas as rich feeding sites teeming with aquatic invertebrates. But the areas also provide resting habitat, and, if adequate upland cover is available, good breeding habitat as well. Waterfowl such as mallard, northern pintail, gadwall, and ruddy duck use such areas (Swanson 1977, Piest and Sowls 1985). In addition, numerous other species, including killdeer, sandpipers, plovers, and common snipe, may be found using these facilities. An investigator in Virginia reported some 27 species of shorebirds and over 150 total species of birds using a local municipal sewage-treatment plant (Middleton 1984).

Hawks and Owls (Birds of Prey)

Hawks and owls are at the top of food chains, and their home ranges are larger than for most other birds considered so far. As a group, these birds have not been studied as much as others in urban areas, but it is probably fair to say that urbanization is more detrimental to them than to most other birds. The more we learn, the better prepared we will be to lessen the impact of urbanization on these birds and to manage for them in metropolitan environments.

One small falcon, the merlin, is proving capable of adjusting to habitat changes brought about by urbanization. Merlins are found throughout North America in open woodlands and grasslands. During the 1960s and 1970s, populations declined as a result of widespread use of the pesticide DDT. Habitat loss over the years has contributed to population declines. Since the early 1970s, however, merlins have been colonizing cities on the Canadian prairies — including Calgary, Edmonton, Moose Jaw, Regina, Saskatoon, and other smaller towns. Biologists first noted the birds in Saskatoon where a single pair nested in 1971. In 1987, 27 pairs nested in the city, the highest recorded nesting density for the species anywhere (James

1988). The birds in Saskatoon have a higher breeding success rate, are less migratory, and appear to be less disturbed by normal human activity than their rural counterparts.

What characteristics make Saskatoon attractive to merlins? The South Saskatchewan River flows through the city and probably provides a corridor for movement of birds into the area. A second key feature seems to be the many spruce trees planted early in the history of the city. Mature trees provide suitable nesting habitat for crows and magpies. Merlins do not build their own nests, but readily use the abandoned nests of crows and magpies in the city (Oliphant and Haug 1985). Thus, the spruce trees provide a critical requirement of the species. Only the older parts of Saskatoon have mature trees offering suitable nesting habitat for the birds. The conifers also provide protective winter cover for the merlins. A third factor contributing to success of Saskatoon merlins is a stable, year-round food supply. House sparrows are abundant and a primary source of food, making up some 70% of the falcon's diet (Oliphant and McTaggart 1977).

Another raptor that appears to be expanding into urban areas is the Mississippi kite (Parker 1987, Glinski and Gennaro 1988). This kite breeds in North America and migrates to Central and South America for the winter. Breeding habitat includes natural grasslands with trees, riparian and upland forests, and human–created shelterbelts, golf courses, and pecan orchards (Glinski and Gennaro 1988). Movement of the birds into urban areas probably is related to an abundant food source (the birds feed mainly on insects), presence of large trees for nesting, and open expanses (such as golf courses) for foraging. Nest predation also may be lower in urban areas. One researcher found twice as many young produced per nesting attempt in urban areas as observed in rural populations reported from other studies (Gennaro 1988a). In rural areas, major predators include other birds, tree squirrels, raccoons, woodrats, and snakes.

The aggressive nature of kites in defending their nest sites is cause for some concern in the urban environment. Aggression is displayed (usually by females) by diving at humans who approach the nest site too closely. The behavior is more prevalent during brooding of young than during incubation of eggs. No physical contact with humans occurs in some 97% of dives, but the degree of aggressiveness varies considerably among different birds (Gennaro 1988b). Human injury is infrequent and usually minor, with stitching of scalp lacerations and treatment for infection reported in some instances (Parker 1987).

Other hawks of wooded urban habitat may include the sharp-shinned, Cooper's, red-shouldered, and red-tailed hawks. The little "sharpie" and Cooper's hawks have smaller territory and home range requirements and are more easy to accommodate in the city. Sharp-shinned hawks are noted for their hunting skills at backyard bird feeders where songbirds are fairly easy prey. The bigger red-shouldered and red-tailed hawks require larger wooded tracts and are more likely to be found in lower-density residential areas of the city.

In more open-land habitat of the city, the small American kestrel and larger peregrine falcon may be found. Kestrels are frequently seen hunting insects and small mammals in grassy open spaces, including roadside rights-of-way. They are cavity nesters, and lack of cavities will restrict populations. As a result, people sometimes erect nesting boxes for these small falcons. Peregrine falcon populations were decimated from wide-scale use of DDT and related pesticides during the 1950s and 1960s. The species is still listed as endangered by the U.S. Fish and Wildlife Service, but populations are on the rebound. The birds are making more and more use of urban habitats where ledges of tall buildings and bridges serve as "artificial cliff" nesting sites. Reproductive success of urban peregrines is similar to that of rural birds. Some 71% of nesting attempts in cities are successful and produce an average of 1.7 young per attempt. In rural areas, 77% of nesting attempts produce 1.9 young per attempt (Cade and Bird 1990). Urban peregrines have a stable food source in the form of pigeons and starlings, although other birds, including waterfowl and shorebirds, also are taken when available (Barber and Barber 1988).

In addition to these daytime predators, there are nocturnal birds of prey (night hunters) that occupy the same trophic level as the hawks but, because they usually hunt by night, fill a slightly different niche. With their large, keen eyes and silent wings, the owls are well adapted to night hunting. Like the hawks, they have been studied little in the urban environment.

The small screech owl is widespread in North America and may be the most abundant of all raptors in suburban areas. Nesting suburban owls in Texas are similar to their rural counterparts with regard to clutch size (about four eggs) and incubation period (about 30 days).

However, suburban owls lay eggs earlier and fledge faster-growing, larger offspring, and density of the suburban owls may be more than three times that of rural birds (Gehlbach 1988). Nest predation in Texas is lower in suburbia, but mortality of adult birds is higher than in rural areas. In southern Connecticut, monthly home ranges of suburban owls vary from 22 to 266 acres (8.8 to 107.5 hectares) and are smallest during December to January and during the nesting period of April to May (Smith and Gilbert 1984).

What factors are responsible for these observed differences between rural and suburban screech owls? Weather in suburbia is typically less variable than in the surrounding countryside, and winter temperatures are generally warmer, both of which may benefit the owl. In Texas, the food supply, including moths, katydids, June bugs, crickets, and earthworms, was estimated to be two to eight times more concentrated in suburbia (Gehlbach 1986). Unfortunately, a contributing factor to higher mortality of adult birds is collisions with vehicles as the owls prey on earthworms on wet road pavements. Although fish are an uncommon source of food for the birds, one researcher documented the capture of goldfish from a patio pond (Prescott 1985)!

Unlike the screech owl and most other owls that hunt by night, the burrowing owl is frequently active during the daytime. This owl is different from most other owls in two other respects. It often nests in loose colonies, and it does so underground!

There are two subspecies of burrowing owl in North America. The "western owl" may be found from western Minnesota, Iowa, Missouri, and Louisiana, northward into lower British Columbia and Manitoba, and southward through lower California and Mexico, into Central and South America (Anderson 1979). The western owl prefers areas of short vegetation and is found in grassland and prairie habitat. It rarely, if ever, digs its own burrow, using instead those dug by ground squirrels and prairie dogs.

The "eastern owl" also inhabits areas of short vegetation, but unlike its western cousin, it digs its own burrow. It breeds throughout Florida and southward into the Bahamas and West Indies (Wesemann and Rowe 1987). Both subspecies appear to be declining. In Florida, the owl is listed as a species of special concern.

Both eastern and western forms have been found residing in urban areas. In 1921, burrowing owls were observed in well-settled parts of

San Diego, California, a city of some 150,000 at the time (Abbott 1930). The birds subsisted wherever there was any extent of vacant land—some even lived in culvert drains of city streets. In addition, a population using some 45 to 50 active burrows was noted in 1963 on the campus of California State University, Sacramento. Unfortunately, the population declined drastically by the early 1970s because of campus expansion and an extensive rodent control program. Dead owls were found in burrows fumigated by campus maintenance personnel for rodent control (Anderson 1979).

In Florida, urbanization continues to open up more and more land, and owls appear to be responding by expanding their range (Wesemann and Rowe 1987). Thus, the process of urbanization, by opening up more land, may be beneficial to the owl, at least in part. Highest owl densities have been recorded in areas 55% to 65% developed. In addition to open land for burrows, food is apparently more abundant at this level of development. More insects have been noted (in response to the diversity and abundance of artificially watered vegetation year-round), and lizards respond to insect abundance. Both are important food items for the owls.

At greater than about 65% development, lizard and insect abundance continues to rise, but numbers of owls do not (Wesemann and Rowe 1987). At this level of development, there may be other environmental and/or behavioral factors limiting owls. For example, increased level of human disturbance—burrow vandalism, pets, and car collisions—may impact the owls. Or, it may be that there is simply insufficient open space remaining. The owls may need some critical minimum area of vacant land to live and reproduce.

Perhaps most cosmopolitan of all owls is the barn owl. In the United States, the species is widely distributed but considered uncommon throughout much of its range. Barn owls are closely associated with humans and their structures, nesting in barns, silos, church bell towers, and other buildings. They are cavity nesters and in nature nest in tree cavities and holes in cutbanks. Lack of nest sites may limit populations. In addition, the birds require grassy foraging habitat containing meadow voles or other small mammals (Colvin 1985), and lack of such habitat also may limit populations.

Nesting barn owls once were present in Columbia, Maryland. Columbia is still under development on land formerly in agriculture and forest. Numerous old barns and other nest sites were destroyed during development, but a few barns and silos were retained and re-modeled for office space and meeting rooms. One silo was used by barn owls as recently as 1976, after the surrounding area was developed. Unfortunately, due to exterior repairs, access holes for the owls were boarded up, preventing further use by the birds. I am unaware of barn owls currently nesting in Columbia.

Other owls, such as the great horned and snowy, may occasionally be found in the metropolitan environment. The large great horned owl is an inhabitant of woodlands. This bird requires substantial forested tracts, and unless some such sites are retained as areas urbanize, these owls will be lost from the bird community. Undeveloped floodplains of larger streams and rivers may provide adequate habitat, even in major cities. Snowy owls are open-land birds, breeding on northern tundra where they prey on lemmings and other small mammals and birds. During winter, they frequently migrate to the northern United States where they may be seen on the outskirts of cities. Since the mid-1960s, a few snowys have regularly wintered on the JFK International Airport at the southwestern end of Long Island, New York (Chevalier 1988).

Mammals

With mammals, as with birds, some general patterns are emerging with regard to use of urban habitat. One rather clear observation is that cities support fewer species of mammals than does the surrounding countryside and that species that do occur in such areas tend to be habitat generalists rather than specialists (VanDruff and Rowse 1986). A few species, mostly exotic ones such as the house mouse and Norway rat, can be abundant in well-developed areas. In less heavily developed areas with some remaining green spaces, other species are more likely to be found. For the following discussion, I have classified mammals ecologically into three groups—small herbivores, large herbivores, and predators. This classification system is in keeping with our earlier discussion of the energy pyramid.

Small Herbivores

Typically, small and medium-sized herbivores (especially granivores) are the most abundant mammals found in cities, towns, and villages.

Deer mice, meadow voles, tree and ground squirrels, chipmunks, rabbits, and woodchucks may be common sights in many urban areas of North America. Based on our understanding of energy flow through ecosystems, we should not be too surprised by this observation.

Among the most visible urban mammals in North America are tree squirrels, particularly the gray squirrel, which is abundant and widespread. Other species, however, may be found. Red squirrels may inhabit northern cities if conifers are present, and in the Midwest, fox squirrels are common park residents. These different species of squirrels have different habitat requirements. Generally speaking, if habitat requirements are met, the squirrels will be present.

Research conducted on the gray squirrel in urban environments indicates that habitat conditions are often good in such areas. An important characteristic of such habitat is the presence of large canopy trees, particularly mast-producing trees such as oaks. These provide food as well as den sites (Hathaway 1973, Flyger 1974, Thompson and Thompson 1980, Williamson 1983). Favorable habitat conditions can result in population densities higher than those found in rural areas. Urban densities of five to six squirrels per acre (12 to 15 per hectare) are fairly common (Flyger 1959, Hathaway 1973), whereas in rural areas, densities of one to two per acre (2 to 5 per hectare) are more typical. Perhaps the highest density anywhere in the United States is in Lafayette Park, adjacent to the White House in Washington, D.C. There, densities have been recorded as high as 20 squirrels per acre (49 per hectare) (Manski et al. 1981). These high densities are due to supplemental feeding by people and many artificial nest boxes located in the park.

Eastern chipmunks, too, may be considered habitat generalists and capable of residing in urban areas if adequate habitat is maintained (Ryan and Larson 1976, Yahner 1987). Remnants of natural stands of deciduous forest are perhaps most ideal, especially if fallen logs and stumps are retained. Also used are stone walls and woodpiles and brush piles. Although I am unaware of research on the subject, some biologists believe that chipmunks are absent from otherwise suitable urban habitat because of heavy predation by domestic cats.

Not all small herbivorous mammals are easily accommodated with increasing urbanization. The salt marsh harvest mouse has become endangered primarily because urbanization has destroyed and modified its habitat (natural tidal marshes) around San Francisco Bay (Shellhammer 1989). The species is dependent on dense cover and utilizes common pickleweed as its preferred habitat. Management of diked marshes may provide the best hope for maintenance of the species.

Large Herbivores

Large herbivores such as pronghorn antelope, elk, and moose are not so easily accommodated in the urban environment as are smaller herbivores. Their size and correspondingly large home ranges generally preclude their use of urban habitats. In most cases, urban development eliminates habitat for these and related species. There are some exceptions, however, with deer the most notable example.

Populations of both white-tailed and mule deer were decimated following settlement of North America by Europeans. This destruction resulted primarily from habitat loss (largely as a result of the cutting of forests followed by agricultural development) and unregulated hunting. However, populations of both species now have been restored because of sound management practices.

As populations of white-tailed deer rebounded, animals began to occupy all suitable habitat. Where travel corridors were present, deer repopulated suitable areas of existing cities. In other locations, deer persisted as urbanization expanded into rural areas. With natural predators eliminated and hunting generally prohibited, many of these urban or suburban populations have become seriously dense.

All, or a major portion, of a whitetail's home range may be within the metropolitan environment. Where food and cover are abundant, home ranges are typically smaller and population densities higher than in rural areas. For example, the metropolitan area of Chicago, Illinois, contains an extensive network of forest preserves that make up some 8.7% of the metropolitan area. Natural predators have been eliminated, and hunting is not allowed. Minimum deer densities range up to 67 deer per square mile (26 deer per square kilometer) (Witham and Jones 1990).

Deer density in Chicago is quite similar to the density of 78 deer per square mile (30 deer per square kilometer) reported for Winnipeg, Manitoba (Shoesmith and Koonz 1977). There, city densities are as high or higher than densities anywhere in Manitoba. Several factors appear to be important in maintaining the Winnipeg herd. One is the close association of winter cover to readily accessible food sources. Native foods include snowberry, red-osier dogwood, chokecherry, rose, and bur oak. In addition, humans provide food in the form of crop residues left in fields, waste hay and grain around riding stables and at a garbage dump, and concentrated alfalfa pellets and powder near a processing plant. Densities up to 168 deer per square mile (65 deer per square kilometer) were recorded on an undeveloped national historic site surrounded by suburban residential housing in New Jersey (Christie et al. 1987). By contrast, deer densities in national forests in Michigan, Pennsylvania, and Wisconsin (states with consistently high deer populations) average about 26 deer per square mile (10 deer per square kilometer) (Trippensee 1948). Even at this density, deer may alter the forest plant community by selectively eating preferred foods and avoiding others. To ensure tree regeneration and desired tree species composition, a density not exceeding 18 deer per square mile (7 deer per square kilometer) may be required (Tilghman 1989).

Throughout the eastern United States there are numerous other examples of high urban–suburban deer populations, including Princeton Township in New Jersey, the suburbs of Philadelphia, and urbanizing sections of northern Virginia. Too little effort has been devoted to managing these populations.

Mule deer inhabit some urban and suburban areas of the western United States, but generally only come into these zones to seek food during severe winters. Such behavior occurs in Rocky Mountain front range communities of Colorado, including Boulder and Denver. Columbian black-tailed deer (a subspecies of mule deer) in suburban habitat near Corvallis, Oregon, however, appear similar to white-tailed deer in their response to residential development. Home ranges are smaller and deer density higher in suburban habitat than in nearby state forest lands (Happe 1982). Other large herbivores seeking food and shelter, such as elk and moose, regularly wander into northern cities during winter.

Aquatic Herbivores

Herbivorous mammals also may inhabit many urban streams, ponds, lakes, and reservoirs of North America. Those most common

During hard winters in northern latitudes, elk sometimes enter towns and
suburbs of cities, seeking food and relief from deep snows. These two animals
were present in a residential area of Banff, Alberta, Canada, and found it to be a
"sanctuary" (even though the designation was not official). (Photo: Sandra K.
Roach.)

and widespread in such areas are the semiaquatic muskrat and beaver.
We know little about the biology and ecology of these animals in the
urban environment. In some instances, urban populations may constitute nuisance or damage situations (chapter 9).

The West Indian manatee is a large aquatic herbivore that may be
found in urban coastal habitat of the southeastern United States. This
tropical species, listed as endangered in the United States, occasionally may be seen north to Georgia and the Carolinas during summer
months but cannot winter north of Florida. Within Florida, it has become more widespread and possibly more abundant during the past
30 years as a result of protection, greater availability of warm water
in winter, and in some areas, increased exotic vegetation (O'Shea
1987). Manatees are commonly observed in Miami, Tampa, Jackson-
ville, and other cities. Such animals may be safer from unlawful per-
secution than those elsewhere in Florida because of close scrutiny by
interested citizens and conservation groups (Moore 1956). On the

down side, however, about one-third of manatee deaths are caused by collisions with boats—and boat traffic is increasing in the state.

In winter, manatees congregate in warmer waters. Such waters may be natural in origin, as is Homosassa Springs, or artificial in nature, as are the warm water effluents of power plants where hundreds of animals live during winter (see O'Shea 1987 for a review). The artificial sources of warm water have encouraged manatees to expand their winter range northward on the Florida coast (Hartman 1979). Thus, because manatees cannot survive cold water temperatures, power plant shutdowns pose a risk for manatees relying on artificial warm water refuges during winter.

Predators

Small and medium-sized predators that may be found in the urban environment include insectivores such as shrews, moles, and many bats, as well as omnivores such as opossum, raccoon, coyote, and fox and carnivores such as mink and weasel.

To my knowledge, practically no research has been conducted on shrews, moles, and bats in urban areas, and consequently we know little about their use of urban habitats. Certainly, shrews and moles are present in yards and other open spaces. Evidence of mole use is most clear because of their characteristic tunnels just below the ground surface. But information on population status, ecology, and natural history of urban moles is lacking.

Bats are found worldwide and are common throughout North America. Of all the mammals, only the rodents exceed them in number of species (Greenhall 1982). As a group, bats are almost entirely beneficial to humans. Natural roosts are caves and tree hollows. A few species, however, readily use structures built by humans, particularly the attics of houses and other buildings. Most bats in the United States and Canada feed primarily on insects, many of which are harmful, and some of these flying mammals consume up to one-half their weight in insects during a night. The little brown bat (commonly found in buildings) feeds on midges, mosquitoes, caddisflies, moths, and beetles. A single bat can easily capture 1,000 insects a night (Tuttle 1979, as cited in Greenhall 1982). In winter, bats migrate or hibernate in caves, mines, and sometimes in houses.

Little is known about bat use of urban habitats, although they are commonly seen flying near streetlights of most cities in the evening. Perhaps they are responding to concentrations of insects drawn to the light. Some evidence indicates that the hunting activity level of big brown bats is similar for urban and rural areas. However, within the urban environment, significantly less activity has been observed in commercial zones compared to residential, over-water, and park habitats (Geggie and Fenton 1985).

We know more about ecology of highly adaptable omnivores such as opossum, raccoon, and coyote in urban areas. From research conducted to date, many of these habitat generalists show higher population densities, smaller home ranges, and less movement in urban areas than in rural areas; they also may be larger bodied and exhibit a higher reproductive rate (Schinner and Cauley 1974, Hoffmann and Gottschang 1977, Hopkins and Forbes 1979, Meier 1983, Slate 1985, and Rosatte et al. 1987). An abundance of food and den sites, and perhaps warmer urban temperatures, probably are important influences.

Raccoons readily exploit new types of cover such as underground storm sewer systems. In and adjacent to Rock Creek Park in Washington, D.C., tree cavities are the most common type of den used in spring through fall, and storm sewers are most common in winter (Manski and Hadidian 1987).

Raccoons eat a wide variety of foods, depending to some extent on availability. In rural areas, vegetable matter generally predominates during most seasons, with corn, cherries, plums, apples, and other fruits and berries eagerly taken as they ripen (Trippensee 1953). Staple animal foods include crayfish, frogs, snakes, and mollusks, although mice, shrews, insects, and earthworms also are taken when preferred foods are scarce. Foods of urban raccoons are quite similar to those eaten by country raccoons, except that dog and cat food and human garbage are more prevalent in the diet of urban animals (Hoffmann and Gottschang 1977, Manski and Hadidian 1987). Cellophane wrappers, string, paper, aluminum foil, bits of plastic, and other such material also have been observed in the fecal droppings of urban raccoons. Densities of urban raccoons may approach one animal per 2.5 acres. In rural areas, one animal per 15 to 45 acres is more realistic (Trippensee 1953). Home ranges of raccoons in metropolitan

Toronto, Ontario, average 0.16 square miles, compared to ranges in rural areas of 4 to 10 square miles (Rosatte et al. 1987).

Opossums may be found in many cities. They eat a wide variety of plant and animal matter including slugs, snails, earthworms, birds, insects, and fruits such as grapes and cherries. Animal matter appears to predominate in urban diets just as in diets of rural animals (Hopkins and Forbes 1980). Like raccoons, opossums make garbage and pet food significant components of their urban diets.

The coyote is becoming more common in urban–suburban settings. Perhaps the most notable urban population occurs in the Los Angeles, California, metropolitan area, which has been inhabited by coyotes at least since the 1930s. Their presence largely results from the topography of the area, although food handouts from people also help to attract and hold the animals. The Santa Susana and San Gabriel mountains to the north and east of the city and the Santa Monica mountains penetrating into the city from the west contain the major populations, estimated to number at least 2,000; some 400 animals or more may reside in the city itself (Gill and Bonnett 1973). The animals find cover in the rugged canyons carpeted with dense, often thorny chaparral. Suburban hillside communities are growing in southern California, restricting coyote habitat and also placing humans in closer contact with these mammals. This activity has resulted in increased loss of small pets to coyotes and even coyote attacks on children. The death of a three-year-old girl in Glendale in 1981 was attributed to a coyote, according to an October 20 article in the *Wall Street Journal*.

Coyotes also inhabit the city of Seattle, Washington. As in Los Angeles, in Seattle the animals are most abundant along the periphery of the city and are closely associated with forest and shrub habitats. Steep, wooded ravines in largely residential north Seattle support the most coyotes (Quinn 1991).

Coyotes are now present in many eastern states and seem to be increasing. They were first sighted in New York in about 1925 and were recorded in Pennsylvania and New Jersey in the 1930s and 1940s. They have been reported in urban areas, too, including Armonk, as well as Rye, and throughout residential Westchester County, New York, all of which are just north of New York City (Yurus 1986).

There is some evidence that urban coyotes have smaller ranges than do rural animals. In the suburbs of Los Angeles, home ranges average 0.4 square miles (1.1 square kilometers) (Shargo 1988). A single yearling male in Lincoln, Nebraska, covered 7.4 square kilometers (2.9 square miles) in its daily activities, whereas adult males in rural areas typically range over 5.6 to 26 square miles (14.5 to 67.8 square kilometers) (Andelt and Mahan 1980, Sargeant et al. 1987).

Although urban coyotes eat many of the same food items as do their rural counterparts, they also consume foods specific to the urban environment. Small mammals, cats, garbage, pet food, and fruit are eaten in suburban Los Angeles (Gill and Bonnet 1973, Shargo 1988). In a suburb of San Diego, California, birds and mammals made up almost 45% of the coyotes' diet. Cottontail rabbits, pocket gophers, blacktail jackrabbits, house cats, and chickens were the most important food items (MacCracken 1982).

Cats may be particularly destructive of ground-nesting birds. The presence of coyotes in southern California canyons on the fringe of development seems to result in fewer gray foxes, domestic cats, and other predators of ground-nesting birds. Apparently, the coyotes help to control the smaller predators, thus indirectly contributing to the maintenance of native, chaparral avifauna diversity (Soulé et al. 1988). There is some evidence that coyotes also displace red foxes in rural areas (Sargeant et al. 1987).

Of the five species of foxes found in North America, the red fox generally is most tolerant of urbanization. Food may consist of natural prey such as mice, squirrels, and rabbits, as well as human garbage. Red foxes prey on moles in my backyard in Columbia, Maryland.

Other small to medium-sized omnivores that may inhabit cities and towns include armadillos and skunks. Armadillos are common in many residential areas of Florida, Texas, and other southern states and appear to be slowly expanding their range northward in the United States. Skunks dig for grubs in backyards and den under porches, decks, and associated structures in residential areas. Home ranges of 0.25 square miles (0.64 square kilometers) are considerably smaller than the 1.2 to 2.0 square miles (3 to 5 square kilometers) used by rural skunks (Rosatte et al. 1987).

True carnivores such as mink and weasel also may inhabit the urban environment, but little is known about ecology and natural history of these mammals in the city.

Large predators such as wolves, mountain lions, and bears (mostly omnivorous) are conspicuously absent from the mammal community of urban habitats. In fact, these predators generally were eradicated even from rural areas by early European settlers of the United States; populations in Canada fared better. Livestock depredations and fear for human safety were largely responsible for such action. In addition, these large predators were viewed as direct competitors with humans for wild game. As a result, the range of wolves in the United States (outside Alaska) now includes only 5% of the area occupied in 1700, and mountain lions remain on no more than 30% of their former range (Robinson and Bolen 1989). Human attitudes toward these large predators appear to be changing. For example, there is widespread and growing interest in restoring wolves to Yellowstone National Park (where they were extirpated by 1927). For all practical purposes, however, these representatives of the food chain cannot be accommodated in urban areas.

Amphibians and Reptiles

Amphibians and reptiles possess characteristics that seem to make them particularly vulnerable to urbanization. They are less mobile than birds and mammals, and thus have more difficulty dispersing to urban habitats once extirpated. This results in localized distributions with many disjunct rather than continuous populations (Cochran 1989). Amphibians and reptiles are poor colonizers.

Birds and mammals are endotherms (they internally regulate their body temperature) and because of the insulating quality of fur and feathers can more easily exploit wide ranges in external temperatures. "Herptiles" (an informal term referring to both amphibians and reptiles) are ectotherms—they depend on the external environment for regulation of body temperature and move in and out of the sun to thermoregulate. This is why turtles, lizards, and snakes bask on logs and rocks. Sometimes the warm pavement of roads and highways attracts these animals, and many are killed by vehicles. Because of their dependence on the external environment for heat, herptiles usually require summer and winter sites (particularly in northern latitudes). Moving between summer breeding ponds and wintering hibernacula may require the crossing of roads and highways and other human obstacles. High mortality may result.

Although many herptiles produce large numbers of eggs, the eggs and young generally are untended. Thus, both egg and hatchling mortality may be high. Some species, such as the gopher tortoise, have low reproductive rates, which compounds the problem. Female gopher tortoises do not reach sexual maturity until 10 to 20 years of age and then only produce a single annual clutch of five to seven eggs (Diemer 1987).

These characteristics result in major impacts by urbanization on amphibians and reptiles. A pattern seems to be emerging that is similar to the one for birds and mammals. Specialized species, for example, the four-toed salamander (which requires natural shallow water habitat such as vernal ponds, bogs, and swamps) and the northern two-lined salamander (which needs cool and flowing spring-fed water), are absent or lacking in urban areas, and species with broad ecological tolerance and more general and simpler habitat needs, for example, the bullfrog and green frog, thrive (Minton 1968, Schlauch 1978, Cochran 1989).

Habitat modification that accompanies urbanization, particularly of aquatic systems, causes the major impact on herptiles (Minton 1968, Orser and Shure 1972, Campbell 1974, Cochran 1989). Many species are totally eliminated when wetlands and associated water habitats are lost due to drainage, channelization, or filling. The scouring of streambeds caused by increased storm-water runoff from urban areas is harmful. In addition, removal of ground cover and underbrush is detrimental to many salamanders and snakes. Urbanization may eliminate 60% or more of the species in an area.

Some species are attracted to constructed ponds and lakes and other habitat features associated with urbanization. Storm-water control impoundments and recreation lakes provide habitat for species such as American and Fowler's toads, gray treefrogs and spring peepers, bullfrogs and green frogs, and snapping and painted turtles (Schlauch 1978, Bascietto and Adams 1983). In addition, some herptiles respond positively to greater food abundance in urban areas (Wesemann and Rowe 1987, Holm 1988). Tree lizards in Tucson, Arizona, are larger bodied and longer lived than lizards in nearby natural desert riparian habitat. Population density and productivity also are higher in the city because of greater food and moisture availability, an extended growing season, reduced risk of freezing, and reduced predation (Holm 1988). American toads and alligator lizards may inhabit residential yards and gardens. The latter species is commonly used in terrariums, a reflection of its resilient nature.

American alligators are found in urban areas of several southeastern states, although the species is not easily accommodated. Urban animals can be a nuisance when they show up in backyard swimming pools or similar areas. Occasionally attacks on people occur. Males seem to travel most and are more frequently found in urban habitats than are females. The species was listed as endangered in 1967 by the U.S. Fish and Wildlife Service, due primarily to overexploitation. However, since that time, populations have increased markedly, and management plans now include regulated harvests in Louisiana, Florida, and Texas (Ruckel 1987, Woodward et al. 1987).

Fish

Urbanization impacts natural fish communities. Typically, watersheds and associated stream and shoreline habitats are modified, contaminants and pollutants increase, waters become warmed and eutrophic (nutrient enriched), storm-water runoff and sediment increase, and humans overexploit any fish resource that may be present (DesJardine 1984). Aquatic impacts seem to be in proportion to the degree of development of watersheds. Actions that can be devastating to natural fish populations and other aquatic organisms include the enclosing of streams in underground culverts, channelization of streams, and construction of dams. These practices eliminate, or greatly reduce, fish habitat and thus fish populations and diversity.

Storm-water runoff increases with urbanization because the vegetated land surface is replaced with buildings, parking lots, streets, and sidewalks—all of which are impervious surfaces. Consequently, precipitation cannot soak into the ground. Instead, it flows into storm drains and from there into nearby streams and rivers. In central Maryland, stream quality impairment was first noted when watershed imperviousness reached 12%, but did not become severe until imperviousness reached 30% (Klein 1979).

Many of the contaminants and pollutants generated by urban development enter aquatic systems through storm-water runoff. Sediment caused by soil erosion, heavy metals, and the nutrients nitrogen and phosphorus generally are most significant (Smith 1982), although other things such as pesticides and oil and grease also may be important.

Sediment in waterways distresses aquatic ecosystems. It reduces the amount of light available to primary producers and slows plant growth (Robel 1961), and the entire food chain is impacted. The importance of aquatic vegetation to water-based ecosystems is now widely appreciated by the public in the Chesapeake Bay region of the eastern United States. The bay is used heavily for both recreational and commercial pursuits, and its watershed now consists mostly of agricultural lands and urban developments. During the 1960s and 1970s, most of the valuable submerged aquatic vegetation was lost. This, along with concern for associated natural resources of the Chesapeake Bay, such as striped bass, oysters, blue crabs, and waterfowl, has led to heightened interest in "Saving the Bay."

Sediment in aquatic systems also scours and abrades stream channels, covers fish spawning sites, and buries benthic (bottom-dwelling) organisms. In addition, it clogs the filters of mollusks (such as clams and oysters) and limits the sight of predators, thereby affecting their ability to sustain themselves.

Eutrophication of urban waters is enhanced as nitrogen and phosphorus contained in lawn fertilizer find their way into aquatic systems. These nutrients stimulate rampant, unwanted aquatic plant growth, particularly algae, which can grow on the surface of water where there is sufficient light. Excessive algal growth is aesthetically displeasing to many people, but also may cause other problems. When algae die, they undergo decay and decomposition, removing dissolved oxygen from the water in the process. A result may be insufficient oxygen remaining to sustain fish and other aquatic organisms.

Modified stream habitat of urban areas generally results in a loss of species diversity and the replacement of cold-water fish such as trout with warm-water fish such as sunfish and carp. A researcher studying streams in central Maryland found that five of nine urban streams were devoid of fish life. Three of the four remaining streams were dominated by the blacknose dace, a species that can tolerate a wide range of environmental conditions (Klein 1979).

In an effort to make up for the loss of fishery resources in urban areas, many state fisheries agencies and a number of Canadian provinces artificially stock urban waters (Duttweiler 1975). Stocking of trout in early spring is a common practice, although winter stocking (for ice fishing) also is done (Carl et al. 1976, Hudson 1984, Wisconsin Department of Natural Resources 1985 as cited in Robinson and Bolen 1989). In recent years, spring stocking of lakes in Columbia, Maryland, has been practiced with considerable angler interest. Most fish stocked under these programs are caught before summer, when water temperatures rise too high for fish to survive.

Invertebrates

To this point in our discussion of animal populations and communities we have focused on vertebrates (animals with backbones). Indeed, these are the animals that most readily come to mind when we think of wildlife. However, invertebrates (animals without backbones) are much more numerous than vertebrates and must not be ignored. Earthworms, spiders, and insects such as dragonflies, damselflies, grasshoppers, crickets, bees, ants, and butterflies are examples of this diverse group. There are far more insects than all other animal groups combined, and the average suburban lawn may contain over 100 species of insects (Falk 1977).

The many invertebrates that occur in urban areas rightly can be considered urban wildlife. They are important links in urban food chains and webs. Bees pollinate flowers; earthworms loosen, aerate, mix, and enrich the soil; and the group as a whole serves as a food base for other organisms from birds to bears. Robins are consumers of earthworms on suburban lawns, and bluebirds feed on grasshoppers and other species. In fact, most birds during the breeding season are heavily dependent on insects and other invertebrates for added protein, calcium, and other nutrients. This is particularly true for egg-laying females and rapidly growing hatchlings. For a period of time, young birds are fed a steady diet of high protein invertebrates.

Some insects in backyards and gardens, such as butterflies, have aesthetic appeal much as do songbirds and are now popular in large zoo displays. Others are considered pests and can cause damage or create nuisances. Termites destroy wooden structures, and mosquitoes can be a nuisance as well as a health hazard sometimes.

Urbanization destroys, modifies, and creates habitat for invertebrates, as we have seen that it does for other animal groups (Frankie and Ehler 1978, Singer and Gilbert 1978). Habitat destruction has greatest impact on specialized species with narrow requirements. For example, urbanization has destroyed or degraded about 99% of the sand dune ecosystem in southern California (Arnold and Goins 1987). This has had a devastating impact on the El Segundo blue butterfly, a specialized species of the sand dunes, classified as an endangered species in 1976. Both the adult and immature forms of the butterfly feed only on the flowers of the seacliff buckwheat, a native perennial shrub that has been destroyed with urbanization and the introduction of exotic annual grasses and ground covers for landscaping.

Modified habitat and created habitat result from a variety of human practices. Landscape plantings, stored grains and other food products, waste products such as garbage, and even buildings, bridges, and other structures provide habitat for insects (Frankie and Ehler 1978). Species richness in urban areas is closely related to environmental heterogeneity. There is some evidence of a pattern similar to that discussed earlier for birds. For example, researchers in northern Virginia found that urbanization of a watershed had little effect on total insect numbers but did have a marked effect on species composition. The relative abundance of Diptera (the insect order in which entomologists group flies) increased at more highly urbanized sites, and these increases mainly consisted of midges. Most other insects decreased, including mayflies, stoneflies, and beetles (Jones and Clark 1987).

Well-landscaped suburban lawns and gardens will support simple food webs. Plants may be fed on by aphids and leafhoppers that provide food for the larvae of hoverflies and ladybird beetles that, in turn, are preyed upon by parasitic insects (Falk 1976, Owen 1978). Or, plants may be fed on by caterpillars of butterflies that, in turn, are fed on by parasitic insects. Various bird species may be present, feeding on both larval as well as adult forms of insects.

Well-landscaped lawns and gardens that have a diversity of plants of known habitat value will support a great variety of insects and other invertebrates. One small English garden supported 21 of the 70 known butterfly species in Britain as well as numerous other insects (Owen 1978). Indeed, butterfly gardening is becoming a popular practice that assists butterfly populations.

Chapter 6

Habitat Patterns in the Landscape

Through activities such as farming, ranching, logging, and construction of cities, towns, and villages, humans have greatly altered the landscape of North America. In colonial times, the once-vast eastern deciduous forest stretched from the Atlantic Ocean to Ohio, and the tallgrass and shortgrass prairies beyond extended to the Rocky Mountains. Today, as one flies over this area on a clear day, the changes are striking. The immense forest is now fragmented into small tracts interspersed among farmlands and metropolitan areas crisscrossed by an array of roads and highways. The tallgrass prairie of Indiana, Illinois, Iowa, and other midwestern states is gone; in its place are corn and soybeans as far as the eye can see. The shortgrass prairie of the Great Plains is now farmed for production of small grain such as wheat and used as rangeland for domestic livestock. Only scattered remnants of prairies remain as isolated patches surrounded by a sea of agriculture.

These changes in the landscape have had a profound effect on wildlife. Some species, for example, the passenger pigeon, became extinct. Others, such as the American bison and prairie chicken, were greatly reduced in number. However, a number of species, including the American pronghorn antelope and wild turkey, have been restored to abundance through careful management following serious population reductions.

There is little doubt that the human population will continue to increase, urbanize, and alter the landscape, and history has shown that more people means less wildlife. Since about 1850 in central Europe, the ratio of bird species lost to species gained has been about two to one (Bezzel 1985). This loss of diversity is attributed to loss of natural habitat, caused primarily by intense human use of the landscape for cities, towns, and villages and for agricultural production. In former West Berlin, Germany, more than half of the native plant and animal species are endangered or already extinct (Sukopp and Weiler 1988). I am sure the same could be said for many other cities of the world.

From the discussion in chapter 2, you might correctly conclude that there is an ecological reason for this. For all practical purposes, life-sustaining energy comes from the sun and flows through food chains and webs consisting of millions of species. At each step up the food chain there is a conversion of energy, some of which is lost from the system, resulting in less and less available energy at progressively higher steps. At every step, an amazing array of species has evolved to fill specific niches—making use of all available energy. Thus, the phrase "Nature abhors a vacuum" is quoted often by ecologists.

Humans, too, use some of the available energy in this "energy pyramid." Ten thousand years ago there were about 5 million people on earth. By 1650 A.D. the number had risen modestly to 500 million. Since that time, however, the human population has mushroomed to today's estimated 5.3 billion, and many authorities point out that controlling our own population is a prerequisite to conserving other life forms. The logic of this argument is based on the fact that an expanding human population uses more and more of the limited supply of energy. It is estimated that humans tie up 20% to 30% of the available energy in terrestrial ecosystems (Wright 1990). If the human population increases to a projected 6.1 billion by the year 2000, its share of energy will likely reach 24% to 37%. As a consequence, even less energy will be available for other species, resulting in population reductions and perhaps further extinction of species. Based on review of the scientific evidence, conservationist Norman Myers (1988) reported that the present-day extinction rate (resulting almost entirely from human modification of the landscape) is at least hundreds of times higher than the long-term natural rate.

Maintaining the earth's biological diversity is a key objective of conservation. Given the evidence of the detrimental impact of an increasing human population on other species, how can we halt or slow the disturbing trend of continued reductions in populations of other species and loss of other life forms on earth while sustaining human life and development? One method, perhaps, is through the application of knowledge gained from landscape ecology. Landscape ecology is an approach to the study of the landscape that interprets landscape as supporting both natural and cultural systems (Vink 1983). Thus, it involves "natural landscapes" as well as "human-dominated landscapes." Habitat patterns or mosaics in the landscape, along with the influence of surrounding areas, are the focus of attention. Perhaps through ecological landscape planning and design, and wise management, we can continue the process of urbanization while doing a better job of conserving wildlife and wildlife habitat.

Landscape Patterns

Many factors contribute to the value of certain habitats for different species of wildlife. Basic habitat types, such as forest, wetland, or grassland, influence the kind of species that will be present. Plant species composition and the age and structure of the plant community also are important. In addition, the size and configuration of any given habitat are significant as is the nature of surrounding land uses. In this section, we are particularly interested in the latter factors—the habitat patterns or mosaics in the landscape; their size, configuration, and relation to one another; and the nature of surrounding land use. All scales are important, from small human-dominated pocket parks and their surroundings in city centers to large tracts of wilderness little used by humans.

In the urban complex particularly, where natural habitats are fragmented and isolated, scattered habitat reserves and interconnecting corridors are especially valuable. Broadly viewed, wildlife reserves consist of variously designated areas such as wildlife refuges, sanctuaries, and preserves, as well as undesignated areas of differing sizes that meet the basic needs of wildlife. The latter category includes parks, cemeteries, and community open spaces. In this discussion, corridors are linear strips of habitat that serve as travel lanes for seasonal movements of wildlife and as interconnecting links between or among habitat reserves. These may be natural, such as ridgetops and riparian strips along rivers, or constructed, such as fencerows and hedgerows.

The conceptual focal point in design of habitat reserves and corridors is island biogeography theory, which was proposed originally for explaining numbers of species on oceanic islands (MacArthur and Wilson 1967). According to the theory, the number of species present on any given island is determined by equilibrium between immigration rates and extinction rates, both of which are influenced by island size and distance to the mainland (a measure of degree of isolation). More species are expected on larger islands (compared to smaller ones) and on islands closer to the mainland (compared to more distant islands).

The theory has been applied to terrestrial "habitat islands" and has some research support. The size, configuration, and spatial arrangement of habitat reserves, and the effectiveness of corridor linkages of urban habitat patches with rural surroundings, affect wildlife use. A number of studies in urban areas show that larger habitat patches support more species than do smaller ones (Table 7). Not only do numbers of species decrease with smaller islands, but species composition also changes (Fig. 6). In forested areas, woodland species such as worm-eating, Kentucky, and hooded warblers are replaced by edge species such as gray catbird, brown thrasher, and indigo bunting.

Over the years, humans have increased the amount of edge by fragmenting natural habitats. Such practice has benefited game species such as grouse, quail, pheasants, cottontails, and deer, although bird-watchers know that more songbirds can be seen along edges, too. These observations were noted many years ago by Aldo Leopold when he formulated a "law of dispersion" stating that the density of those wildlife species requiring two or more habitat types is proportional to the amount of edge between or among those habitat types (Leopold 1933).

Edges are still important today. Many waterfowl populations in North America are at all-time lows, and most of these prefer the small prairie potholes with more edge during the breeding season. In addition, modern farming practice tends toward ever-larger fields, with proportional loss of hedgerows. Increases of edge habitat in these situations are desirable. However, natural habitats now have been fragmented to such a degree that creating more edge frequently is less important than creating and maintaining large blocks of habitat for those dwindling native species that require such habitat. Neotro-

Table 7. Predicted numbers of species for urban terrestrial "habitat islands" of different sizes (Reprinted, by permission of the publisher, from Adams and Dove 1989.)

Island size (hectares)	Woodland birds[a]	Woodland birds[b]	Woodland birds[c]	Chaparral birds[d]	Land verte- brates[c]	Urban parks[e] Flies	Urban parks[e] Beetles
1	–	–	6.4	1.6	8.7	–	–
2	–	24.0	13.8	2.5	13.5	–	–
4	13.0	27.0	21.2	3.4	21.0	25.2	6.6
8	21.0	31.0	28.6	4.3	32.8	29.7	7.7
12	27.0	33.0	32.9	4.8	42.5	32.6	8.5
16	29.0	36.0	36.0	5.2	51.1	34.9	9.0
20	31.0	37.0	38.3	5.5	58.9	36.8	9.5
24	31.5	39.0	40.3	5.7	66.2	38.4	9.9
30	32.5	40.0	42.7	6.0	76.4	40.5	10.4
36	33.0	42.0	44.6	6.2	85.8	42.2	10.8
42	33.5	43.0	46.2	6.4	94.7	43.8	11.2
65	–	48.0	–	7.0	–	48.5	12.3
100	–	–	–	7.5	–	53.7	13.6
200	–	–	–	–	–	63.2	15.8
300	–	–	–	–	–	69.5	17.3

Note: One hectare = 2.47 acres.
[a]Estimated from Figure 2 of Luniak (1983).
[b]Estimated from Figure 2 of Tilghman (1987).
[c]From Vizyová (1986).
[d]From Soulé et al. (1988).
[e]From Faeth and Kane (1978).

pical migrants such as warblers, thrushes, tanagers, and vireos are not adapted to edges. These birds are on the breeding grounds in temperate North America for only a short time, three to four months each year (Robbins 1991). Most lay only one clutch of eggs, tend to build open nests, and tend to nest on or near the ground. All of these characteristics make the birds more susceptible to nest predation by blue jays, common crows, raccoons, skunks, and similar predators hunting along edges. These predators are well adapted to edge habitat.

These nesting characteristics also make forest interior birds in eastern North America more susceptible to nest parasitism by cowbirds. The cowbird lays its eggs in the nests of other species, the parents of which then raise cowbirds at the expense of their own young (Brit-

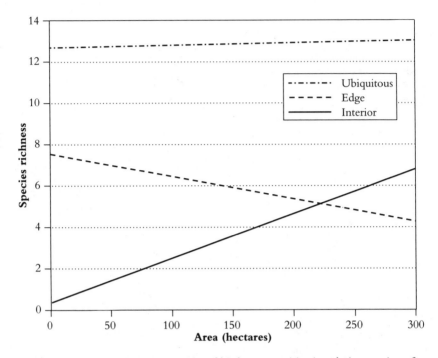

Figure 6. Changes in the composition of bird communities in relation to size of deciduous forest habitat islands in the eastern United States. Populations of many forest birds are declining, and fragmentation of forests into smaller and smaller blocks is a major contributing factor. (One hectare = 2.47 acres.) (Source: Adams and Dove 1989 after Whitcomb et al. 1981.)

tingham and Temple 1983). Cowbirds are open-land birds and historically inhabited the vast prairies of North America. However, with increasing fragmentation of the eastern deciduous forest, populations are growing and expanding in the East.

Both predation and parasitism take the greatest toll on forest interior birds within 328 feet (100 meters) of a forest edge (Robbins 1991). Thus, interior birds inhabiting small forest tracts are more vulnerable to predation and nest parasitism than are birds in larger forests. For example, the center of a square 10-acre (four hectare) forest tract would be within 328 feet (100 meters) of edge on all four sides. Reserves of this size or smaller are of little value to forest interior birds.

Corridors connecting habitat reserves increase the value of those reserves for wildlife. The usefulness of small woodlots to breeding forest birds is enhanced if such woodlots are near larger wooded reserves and connected to the latter by corridors (MacClintock et al. 1977). Forest birds and small mammals use fencerows between woodlots much more than they travel across open fields (Wegner and Merriam 1979). In Great Britain, red foxes regularly use railroad corridors to travel in and out of towns and cities (Kolb 1985).

In summary, habitat size and configuration affect wildlife populations. For a given size, a nearly round or square reserve will be of greater value to woodland species than will a long, narrow reserve. The latter would have more edge, and thus less importance to woodland species but greater value to edge species. By knowing how different species and groups of species respond to different habitat sizes and patterns, we are better able to manage for them.

Ecological Landscape Planning and Design

Given what we know about how different species of wildlife respond to different sizes and patterns of habitat, how can ecological landscape planning and design be undertaken? As a first step, a conservation strategy must be developed for wildlife in urban and urbanizing areas. The strategy should emphasize regional species diversity—those native species of natural habitats within geographical regions. It also must relate to human needs and desires. A focus on preservation and incorporation of regionally limited and/or unique habitat types in a network of continuous open space is important (Leedy et al. 1978, Noss and Harris 1986). An early requirement is to identify habitats and determine their relative value for wildlife (Fig. 7). This implies that some areas are more valuable than others and that development will occur.

The identification and evaluation of habitats require tough choices. How do we decide which habitats are most valuable? Certainly critical habitat for threatened or endangered species should receive high priority. Also high on the list should be regionally limited or unique habitats and habitats that support large numbers of native animals or provide exceptional species diversity (Burns et al. 1986, Byers et al. 1987). These areas would constitute core reserves (Fig. 8) and would be set aside as wildlife sanctuaries, perhaps allowing scientific nature study, but restricting minimum management activity.

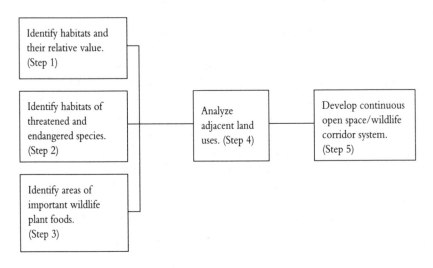

Figure 7. Flow diagram of basic wildlife planning procedures at the regional level. Adhering to these guidelines will help to minimize detrimental impacts of development on wildlife. (Source: Leedy et al. 1978.)

Core reserves should be connected to other reserves or adjacent natural habitat with corridors, resulting in an integrated network of habitat. Buffer zones provide transition areas between core reserves and urban development. One or more such zones will help to maintain the naturalness and ecological function of core reserves while providing for human use and enjoyment as well.

Cluster-type housing development offers greater flexibility for maintaining some of the natural land features and habitats than does traditional-type development. Lot sizes, setback requirements, and road rights-of-way typically are reduced, and development is grouped on the most buildable portions of a site with the remainder preserved as open space. For example, 1,000 acres (405 hectares) of valuable riparian habitat was slated for single-family detached housing in the developing city of Columbia, Maryland. Local citizens, including knowledgeable biologists, convinced the developer and local authorities that the area should be preserved. As a result, the development plan was modified, slightly increasing planned housing density elsewhere in Columbia in order to preserve this natural area. The site now not only will retain its value to numerous wildlife species,

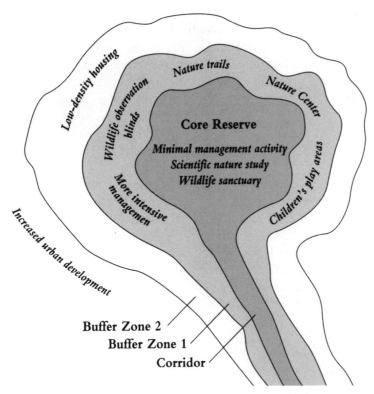

Figure 8. An urban wildlife reserve, connecting corridor, and buffer zones providing multiple benefits. Incorporating reserves and corridors in the development design will help to sustain wildlife populations and other natural environmental quality values important to human well-being. (Reprinted, by permission of the publisher, from Adams and Dove [1989] after Harris [1984] and Noss [1987]. See also Goldstein et al. [1981, 1983], Hoehne [1981], Shaw et al. [1986], Hench et al. [1987], Schicker [1987], and Tilghman [1987].)

but also will be of exceptional value to people. It will be used as an environmental study area for school children, and adults will have access to the nature trails and other facilities and programs as well.

From a practical standpoint, a number of methods can be used to acquire and protect natural areas of value as urban wildlife reserves and corridors. These include outright land purchase, various tax incentive programs, local, state, and federal laws, and voluntary registration of sites as wildlife reserves by the landowner (Adams and Dove 1989).

Once landscape habitat patterns are established, the wildlife biologist turns his or her attention to habitat management. Most habitats are in a continual state of change, and management is needed to maintain desired conditions. The once-vast prairies of the Midwest and Plains States originally were maintained by lightning fires that swept through the grasslands about every three to five years. Fire invigorated native grasses — big bluestem, little bluestem, switchgrass, and Indian grass — and suppressed woody growth. The animal community associated with prairies was dependent on fire to maintain prairie habitat.

Prairie reserves established today also must be managed to suppress woody growth, and planned and carefully controlled fires are an effective management tool. Fire as a management tool is most used in rural areas, but there are examples of its use in the metropolitan environment: The Rock Island State Botanical Preserve in Cedar Rapids, Iowa, is periodically burned to maintain native prairie habitat. There are other techniques and approaches that can be used to manage urban habitats for wildlife. Let's now turn our attention to these.

Chapter 7

Aspects of Wildlife Management

Wildlife management, whether practiced in rural or urban areas, involves manipulation of animal populations and habitats to preserve species as well as to provide wildlife resources for human needs. One may wonder why management is necessary at all. Why not just "let nature take its course"? An important point in this regard is that human influence on earth is pervasive. To one degree or another, we have impacted wildlife habitats from the Arctic to the Antarctic, and it now appears that some level of management is needed for most habitats. Sound management was instrumental in restoring game species to abundance in the United States (Kallman et al. 1987). Unregulated hunting and loss of habitat that progressed into the early 1900s devastated many populations. But white-tailed deer, wild turkey, wood duck, pronghorn antelope, and others have rebounded to the extent that many game species in the United States are now thriving.

Management also is vital to restoring populations of endangered species. The bald eagle and American alligator are well along the road to recovery. In fact, urban alligators are now so numerous in some Gulf Coast communities that control measures are needed to restrict population growth. The peregrine falcon, which utilizes tall buildings and bridges as artificial cliffs in urban areas, as well as more natural habitat in the surrounding countryside, also is responding well to management. However, there are other species, including the California condor, Kirtland's warbler, whooping crane, and black-footed ferret, that are extremely endangered. Only time will tell if we are knowledgeable enough and have the will and resources to restore these species.

So-called "nongame" species represent a third group of wildlife that requires management. This group is made up of species, such as the wood warblers mentioned earlier, that are neither hunted as game nor endangered. Nonetheless, populations are declining and many species in this group need attention.

In some situations, certain species may become a nuisance or cause property damage. Too many blackbirds, geese, or deer may cause significant crop loss for farmers. Bats or squirrels in the attic or raccoons in the chimney of one's home may be unacceptable and require human intervention.

First, a management strategy, with a well-defined objective, is required to effectively manage wildlife. The management objective must focus on the requirements of desired species or communities as well as on the attitudes and goals of the landowner or public. Is the aim to increase, to decrease, or to maintain populations at a given level? In working with populations, biologists attempt to determine the biological carrying capacity of the habitat and to maintain populations at or below this level. Population densities maintained above the carrying capacity for very long will lead to habitat destruction. Too many white-tailed deer in an urban park will overbrowse the area, decimating their own food source and destroying the habitat of many other species. The population density that is acceptable to people also is an important factor to be weighed.

The management objective must identify whether selected species or entire communities are the focus of attention. Wildlife management in the early history of European settlement of North America focused on individual game species such as deer and turkey because populations of these species were greatly reduced from habitat loss and unregulated hunting and because game species were of primary importance to people at the time. Management for selected game species remains an important objective on many public and private lands throughout North America. Species management also is paramount when dealing with endangered species. Recently, however, increased attention has focused on habitat or community management: management of the entire assemblage of species in a given area. In community management, efforts generally aim to maintain natural or near-natural conditions to support the diversity of wildlife present in the area prior to human settlement. National parks and wilderness areas are good examples of lands where community management is a primary objective.

Second, an effective management strategy must consider the biology and ecology of species. One must know the basic needs of wildlife—the food, cover, water, and space requirements. These vary for different species, and biologists understand the requirements for relatively few species. Lack of knowledge concerning the biology and ecology of species makes management difficult.

Third, an effective management strategy must consider and evaluate different approaches to wildlife management. Generally, management activity falls into one of the following categories: passage of protective regulations, establishment of refuges, control of predators, restocking/transplanting, feeding, erection of nesting structures, and habitat management.

Regulations and Local Ordinances

Regulation of hunting was an early and effective wildlife management technique in the United States that notably assisted restoration of game species. The setting of hunting seasons and bag limits is still used today by state and federal wildlife agencies. In addition, a variety of federal and state law and regulation dealing with land uses affect wildlife. Examples at the federal level include the Fish and Wildlife Coordination Act (1934), Land and Water Conservation Act and Wilderness Act (both originally passed in 1964), National Environmental Policy Act (1969), and the Surface Mining Control and Reclamation Act (1977).

In metropolitan areas, local ordinances also can impact wildlife and wildlife habitat. Zoning ordinances have a profound effect on wildlife habitat. Large-lot, residential zoning on the order of two to three acres (0.8 to 1.2 hectares) is particularly destructive. Such development sprawls structures over the landscape, fragmenting natural habitats and lessening their value to regional native species. This type of suburban residential development has been used extensively in the past and is still employed today. However, better approaches are available and being used across the country, such as cluster zoning. As a result, the most valuable wildlife habitat can be preserved as open space and interconnecting links can be retained or created to minimize detrimental impact on wildlife.

Local zoning that incorporates wildlife considerations is being used in Teller County, Colorado, a developing residential suburb of Colorado Springs. There, a natural resource zoning ordinance requires consideration of wildlife resources in consultation with the state's Division of Wildlife. Distribution maps for species of concern are prepared and stored in a computer, using geographic information system technology. A composite map can then be generated by stacking the individual species maps. The composite map is reviewed and evaluated for low, moderate, or high impact to wildlife habitat based on projected land use changes. Proposed development in high-impact areas receives greater scrutiny. A conservation plan must be filed with the county planning commission and proposed development may require design modifications. Developments in moderate-impact areas usually are mitigated by minor adjustments, and projects in low-impact areas do not require any special measures by the developer (Bissell et al. 1987).

Zoning is used to protect wetlands in Connecticut, where strong local wetland ordinances supplement state and federal regulations. All but 13 of the state's 169 towns regulate wetlands at the local level (Aurelia 1987). For example, the Greenwich zoning ordinance includes a planned residential zone and a conservation zone, both providing some flexibility for development alternatives in protecting wetlands and water courses.

Weed and grass control ordinances of county and municipal governments also affect wildlife habitat. These laws generally require the residential property owner to keep herbaceous vegetation of lawns below 12 to 15 inches (30 to 38 centimeters). Homeowners interested in natural landscaping and creating meadows in their backyards, with wildflowers such as black-eyed Susans and Queen Anne's lace for butterflies, meadowlarks, goldfinches, and other wildlife, frequently run up against these ordinances. In some cases, courts have ruled in favor of the homeowner. A circuit court judge in Virginia struck down Fairfax County's weed and grass ordinance, finding that "[the ordinance] is an unreasonable, arbitrary and excessive exercise of the County's police powers which bears no relation to public health, safety, morals or general welfare" (*Board of Supervisors of Fairfax County, Virginia v. Wills and Van Metre, Inc.*—At Law No. 35094,

Nineteenth Judicial Circuit of Virginia, 14 September 1976.) In Little Rock, Arkansas, a judge dismissed a citation against a local resident because the citizen's "overgrown" yard was legally certified as a "backyard wildlife area" by the Arkansas Fish and Game Commission (*City of Little Rock, Arkansas v. Lynda Lynn Sain Allison*—No. 89-10401, Little Rock Municipal Court, 1 January 1990).

Local ordinances may relate to other issues that influence wildlife. Many local jurisdictions, in addition to states, now require management of storm water, an action that has bearing on wetland wildlife as well as other species. Ordinances exercising some control over free-running cats and dogs are common throughout the United States. Also, local laws may apply to wildlife feeding. In the fall of 1991, residents of Plymouth, Massachusetts, voted to ban waterfowl feeding on a city pond. Feeding attracts and holds large concentrations of birds that can become a nuisance.

Refuges, Preserves, Sanctuaries

Refuges, preserves, sanctuaries—all three names are given to places established to provide safe havens for wildlife from natural and human-related mortality factors. In addition, they serve wildlife as bases for population expansion into surrounding habitat and provide people with opportunities for wildlife observation and enjoyment. Refuges may be established to protect a single species or to provide habitat for conserving a biotic community. President Theodore Roosevelt is credited with establishing the first federal bird sanctuary in 1903 to protect nesting herons and egrets from feather hunters. Women's feathered hats were fashionable at the time, and the best feathers came from birds in breeding plumage. By executive order, Roosevelt set aside Pelican Island in Florida—the forerunner of the national wildlife refuge system that now includes more than 430 units.

Although most effort has gone to establishing refuges in rural areas, such sanctuaries also can be set up in cities, towns, and villages. They can range in size from backyards to large city parks to even larger state and federal grounds. Between these extremes, urban refuges can be established in community and neighborhood open spaces, vacant lots, or institution grounds of churches, hospitals, and schools. Frequently such refuges are established to protect natural ar-

Urban parks and refuges provide wildlife and environmental education opportunities to city youth. Lacking areas nearby, many kids are deprived of such experiences. (Photo: J. R. Frye, U.S. Fish and Wildlife Service.)

eas from encroaching development, but refuges that are not natural, that are completely designed and created are valuable, too. An early example of the former is Lake Merritt, a triangular body of salt water in the city of Oakland, California. Lake Merritt has provided sanctuary to wintering waterfowl species such as pintail, shoveler, canvasback, scaup, and ruddy duck since its establishment in 1869 as the state's first game refuge (Dixon 1927). It is now largely surrounded by housing but continues to serve as a winter refuge for wildlife.

Several national wildlife refuges are excellent urban sanctuaries. Bayou Sauvage encompasses more than 18,000 acres (7,200 hectares) of wetlands within the city limits of New Orleans, Louisiana. It is a wintering ground for some 90,000 ducks and coots and includes two bird rookeries with glossy ibis, snowy egrets, great egrets, white ibis, and great blue herons. Minnesota Valley is a 12,000-acre urban green corridor along a 34-mile (55-kilometer) stretch of the Minnesota River on the outskirts of Minneapolis–St. Paul. The area is managed to provide for a diversity of plants and animals. In California, some 19,000 acres (7,700 hectares) of salt marshes, upland, tidal mudflats, and open water constitute the San Francisco Bay refuge, which is surrounded by an urban population of 5 million people. About 250 species of birds use the bay, including large numbers of shorebirds and waterfowl. It is a key wintering area for diving ducks along the Pacific Flyway, the established air route of migratory waterfowl along the western coast of North America.

Other notable urban wetland refuges include Jamaica Bay in New York City (virtually at the end of the airport runway) and Tinicum Marsh, on the outskirts of Philadelphia, Pennsylvania. Jamaica Bay, administered by the National Park Service, consists of 9,155 acres (3,708 hectares) of saltwater bay, salt marsh, tidal flats, and scattered islands. It is an excellent stopover for birds in migration, and it is not uncommon to see 90 species of birds there each day during the spring or fall migration (Morris 1989). Numerous waterfowl, shorebirds, and marsh birds use the refuge, and 37 species of warblers have been recorded there. The total number of bird species observed over the years is more than 300. Some 200,000 people visit the refuge annually.

Tinicum Marsh, administered by the U.S. Fish and Wildlife Service, is the largest remaining tidal wetland in Pennsylvania, and more than 280 bird species have been seen there. It also provides habitat for opossum, raccoon, and muskrat, and is one of the few places in Pennsylvania where the endangered red-bellied turtle and southern leopard frog can be found (Anonymous 1989).

A metropolitan wildlife refuge system is evolving in the Portland, Oregon–Vancouver, Washington area and is coordinated by the regional Metropolitan Service District (Houck 1991). Local governments are involved from the four participating counties as is virtually every city in the metropolitan region. The refuge system will link a mosaic of natural areas as green spaces for wildlife and people alike.

Predator Control

Human fear of large predators such as wolves and cougars, and concern for the safety of domestic livestock and wild game, led to the eradication of these predators from state after state as settlement pushed westward in the United States. Other predators also were destroyed routinely, including hawks, owls, and eagles. State and federal wildlife agencies sanctioned predator control as a way of increasing game populations. It was common practice in the early 1900s for state and local authorities to pay bounties on such predators as wolves, foxes, coyotes, and weasels. The practice was later discontinued as it proved ineffective and wasteful of taxpayers' money.

Predator control is still practiced, however. In the western United States, coyotes particularly are targeted under the auspices of livestock protection, and red foxes are removed from northern marshes managed for waterfowl production. Other examples could be cited, but the practice is not as widespread and indiscriminate as it once was. Human attitudes toward predators are slowly changing to recognize that these animals play an important functional role in ecosystems.

In urban areas, some native predators, particularly the larger ones, have been eliminated. However, many other species may still be found. Predaceous aquatic invertebrates, including water striders and larvae of dragonflies and damselflies, and terrestrial ones, such as ambush bugs and assassin bugs, may be present. Spiders, too, are found, along with insect-eating frogs and toads, birds such as purple martins and swallows, and mammals such as shrews and bats. Even some hawks and owls may survive. A few predators are encouraged. For example, martin houses and bat houses are erected to enhance populations of these insect eaters.

Control of wild predators generally is not necessary in the urban environment, but this may not be the case for predatory domestic pets, particularly dogs and cats. In 1990, there were some 54.5 million pet dogs and 63.2 million pet cats in the United States (Pet Food Institute 1990). In addition to pets, there are feral or free-ranging animals. Populations of these predators are sustained at high levels through food and shelter supplied by humans. Although largely dependent on humans, many animals roam freely, particularly cats. Nonetheless, free-running dogs (both strays and pets) also are present in many urban areas. In Baltimore, Maryland, these carnivores have been estimated at 450 to 750 per square mile (174 to 290 per square kilometer) (Beck 1974). Beck noted some predation on rats and birds but found that most food came from garbage and handouts.

Cats may have more impact than dogs on wildlife in metropolitan areas. Cat owners who let their pets roam freely out-of-doors sooner or later find them returning with captured mice, field voles, and birds.

Little study of urban cat ecology has occurred in North America. Population densities of pet cats have been estimated at 1.8 animals per acre (Fagen 1978), a level much greater than any reported for rural populations. How representative this density is for cities in general is unknown. To this figure one must add the free-ranging population. Again, little information is available on the size of the population, but densities in Brooklyn, New York, have been estimated as high as 2.0 animals per acre (Calhoon and Haspel 1989).

The impact of these predators on wildlife in the urban environment is not well understood. Cats accounted for 24% of the known mortality of a mourning dove population in Berkeley, California (Leopold and Dedon 1983). Laboratory studies suggest that hunger and hunting are controlled by separate neurological centers in the cat brain (Polsley 1975, Adamec 1976). So, even well-fed cats may be efficient predators on wildlife. In England, it is estimated that some 70 million birds and small mammals are killed by cats each year (Churcher and Lawton 1989). Domestic cats may be the major killer of small birds and mammals in the urban–suburban environment in that country. Many biologists believe that cats are particularly destructive of ground-nesting birds and perhaps decimate chipmunk populations in metropolitan areas. Thus, in the highly modified urban environment, where cats and dogs are maintained at levels that could not be sustained in nature, some control of these predators may be necessary if we want to maintain a diverse wildlife community.

Restocking and Transplanting

As used here, the term "restocking" refers to replenishing depleted habitats with native species artificially reared by humans or with captured wild animals transplanted from other areas. In this context, restocking is equivalent to reintroducing extirpated species to areas they once occupied. The technique has wide application in rural as well as urban areas.

Before reintroducing a species, it is important to first determine and correct factors responsible for its extirpation to ensure reestablishment. Present habitat conditions must be suitable for the species. A manager should be satisfied that adequate food, cover, and water are available, and that the available habitat is large enough to sustain a population of the species. Also to be considered are new mortality sources such as automobiles and cats and dogs. Pollution may be higher in the city than in the surrounding countryside, and this factor should be evaluated. Finally, how will the species interact with people? Chipmunks cause few problems in urban areas. On the other hand, as discussed in chapter 5, Mississippi kites may "attack" humans who approach nest sites too closely. This does not necessarily mean that the uncommon kite should not be restocked in urban areas. Rather, greater care must be taken in selection of release sites to minimize any conflict with people. In addition, greater public education efforts may be necessary—pointing out not only the characteristics of the bird but also why it needs protection.

Thought also must be given to the condition of individual animals being reintroduced to ensure that they are healthy and disease-free. In addition, they must be geographically and ecologically suited to the new area, including its temperature and precipitation regimes.

Restocking has been instrumental in restoring the endangered peregrine falcon in eastern North America where populations were devastated from widespread use of DDT in the 1950s and 1960s. In the early 1940s, 275 eyries (nest sites) were located in the United States east of the Rocky Mountains, most of which were east of the Mississippi River (Hickey 1942). In 1964, 133 formerly used sites were checked for occupancy, and none was found active (Berger et al. 1969). The Peregrine Fund initiated a program to reestablish self-sustaining populations of the birds in 1970. The fund pioneered the successful production of peregrines in captivity and their release to the wild. In nature, the birds are cliff nesters. In human-modified environments, however, they are attracted to artificial cliff habitat such as tall buildings, towers, and bridges and to the readily available food source of pigeons, starlings, and other birds. Between 1975 and 1985, 771 young captively reared falcons were released to the wild in Canada and the United States (Cade and Bird 1990). Eighty-eight percent of the 236 birds released in urban areas survived to independence whereas 79% of 535 birds released in rural areas survived. Lower nest mortality at urban sites was due to less predation by raccoons, foxes, and great horned owls.

Cities, however, are not without hazards to the falcons. Birds are killed from collisions with plateglass windows, sides of buildings, and wires. They also are sometimes inadvertently poisoned in pest control programs.

Peregrines seldom nested successfully in North American cities before the 1950s. However, in 1988, 30 to 32 pairs of peregrines were present in at least 24 cities and towns in Canada and the United States (Cade and Bird 1990). Most of these were captively reared and released falcons—some released in urban areas and some in rural areas. There is considerable movement of birds between urban and rural sites. However, it appears that captive-reared birds have a stronger tendency than wild birds to enter the urban environment when released, and to use human-made structures; perhaps such birds are less afraid of humans and their artifacts as a result of a wider variety of early experiences with different, usually artificial, environmental situations (Cade and Bird 1990). These birds are hatched in an incubator, hand-fed in the lab for a few days, parent-reared in a cage, and fed by humans at the release site until self-sufficient.

Restocking urban habitats also has been successful for amphibians and reptiles. The Jamaica Bay Wildlife Refuge in New York City is an excellent wildlife area, noted particularly for the diversity of birds present during migration. Past agricultural development and urbanization of western Long Island, however, devastated native amphibian and reptile populations to the extent that most species were extirpated. Recently, biologists reintroduced 11 species to Jamaica Bay. Before restocking, habitat suitability was carefully evaluated. Also, considerable thought was given to the species that would be translocated, and three basic criteria were followed. One, only species native to Long Island were used. Two, individuals were collected from populations facing extirpation or from those large enough to sustain collection. Three, lower trophic level species were released first as this was necessary to sustain higher level organisms. Of the 11 species restocked, overwinter survival was recorded for ten species and breeding was confirmed for seven (Cook and Pinnock 1987).

Feeding

Providing supplemental food to wildlife is a powerful means of attracting and holding animals in a given area. Species from hummingbirds at backyard feeders to grizzly bears at town garbage dumps will readily make use of such food. This fact has been recognized for a long time. Aldo Leopold (1933) discussed the use of planted food patches and feeding stations to assist overwinter survival of game birds and mammals such as bobwhite, pheasant, cottontail rabbit, and white-tailed deer. Feeding in urban areas has an equally long history. During the winter of 1918-1919, 4 tons (3.6 metric tons) of whole barley were fed to waterfowl in the city parks of Oakland, California; during the winter of 1926-1927, some 19 tons (17.2 metric tons) of barley were fed (Dixon 1927). Today, most biologists discourage this practice, except under special emergency circumstances where natural foods are not available. Such might be the case when sudden extremely cold periods freeze wintering water areas for waterfowl, stranding the birds. Exceptionally deep snows may temporarily immobilize large mammals such as mule deer and elk. Plans should be well thought out for feeding under such emergency conditions.

The reason that feeding is generally discouraged for most wild species is that it alters the behavior of wild animals and tends to concentrate them in a given area above the natural carrying capacity of the land. This has detrimental impact on other species in the system. Deer populations held above the natural carrying capacity of the land by supplemental feeding will overbrowse natural vegetation, destroying habitat components required by the ovenbird, wood thrush, and other species. This is why the National Park Service maintains "no feeding" signs in the national parks. If natural habitat is maintained, animals generally will be present in appropriate numbers. Thus, feeding should be done only after careful consideration. It is most helpful if done in conjunction with habitat enhancement.

Backyard bird feeding is a specialized form of wildlife feeding that is one of the most popular wildlife-associated outdoor recreational activities practiced by Americans. A recent survey in the United States found that more than 82 million Americans feed birds more than 1 billion pounds (450,000 metric tons) of seed annually (U.S. Fish and Wildlife Service 1988). Despite the scope and magnitude of this practice, little research has been conducted on backyard bird feeding. Some information is available on preferences of seeds by different birds. The small, black, oil-type sunflower seed is superior to other seeds for most bird species (Geis 1980). White proso millet also is highly attractive, particularly for the smaller seed eaters such as finches and sparrows. Many seeds commonly found in prepackaged

Bird feeding is the most popular form of wildlife recreational activity in North America. However, little is known about the effects of feeding on bird populations. (Photo: Jay Anderson.)

bags of birdseed are little used by birds. Included in this group are wheat, sorghum, hulled oats, and rice.

The effects of feeding on bird populations are largely unknown. Biologists would like to know more about how feeding might affect the physical condition of birds, population mortality rates, and over-all ecological balance within an area (Brittingham 1991). Some evidence indicates that birds with access to feeders are heavier and better able to survive harsh winters (Brittingham and Temple 1988a).

Concern about mortality centers on disease, predation, and accidental collisions with windows. Wildlife mortality from disease is often difficult to measure because sick animals typically seek secluded cover. However, diseases of most concern are salmonellosis and aspergillosis. Salmonellosis (food poisoning) is a bacterial disease readily spread through feces-contaminated seed at feeders. Its prevalence is related to the kind of species using the feeder and their abundance and to the type of feeder used (Brittingham and Temple 1988b). Gregarious species such as mourning doves, starlings, house sparrows, and goldfinches are most susceptible when feeding in large numbers on platform feeders. Aspergillosis is a fungal disease caused by moldy seed. Keeping platform feeders clean (or using other types of feeders) and not feeding moldy seed are two management recommendations that will help to reduce disease risks at feeders.

Concern about predators generally centers around domestic cats and sharp-shinned and Cooper's hawks. Generally, feeders placed in the open give birds good visibility, and thus reduce surprise attack by cats. However, shrubs and trees should be nearby to provide quick access to cover from attacking hawks.

Some birds are killed in collisions with house windows, after having been attracted to an area by feeders. Clear or reflective glass presents the most serious problem, and birds are more vulnerable to large panes near ground level and at heights above 9.8 feet (three meters) (Klem 1991). Use of nonreflective tinted glass is effective in preventing strikes. Also, netting or other outside glass covering that is opaque or translucent is effective; coverings can partially obscure the window but must be uniformly spaced over the surface. Or, simply placing feeders within one foot (0.3 meters) of the unobscured glass surface will effectively prevent strikes (Klem 1991).

Finally, it is becoming more and more apparent that feeding alters the ecological balance of the bird community, with granivores and omnivores favored over insectivores. For example, blue jay populations increase with feeding. These birds are nest predators of other species, including woodland warblers, a group of birds in need of protection. Exotic species such as house sparrows and starlings also are encouraged by feeding and compete with native species. In addition, some concern relates to the effect of feeding on the distribution and range expansion of birds. With feeding, some species may not migrate as normal. Waterfowl, mourning doves, common flickers, chipping sparrows, and song sparrows may remain north of their traditional wintering grounds. Some southern species, for example, the cardinal and tufted titmouse, appear to be expanding their range northward because of human development and perhaps because of access to feeders. Better understanding of the effects of feeding on bird populations will allow biologists to make better management recommendations regarding this widespread wildlife management practice.

Nesting Structures

Numerous species of wildlife will use artificial nesting structures. Boxes for cavity-nesting birds generally come to mind when considering such structures; boxes also may be used, however, by mammals such as squirrels, raccoons, and bats, as well as by other wildlife. In addition, nesting platforms and baskets are used by some species that are not hole or cavity nesters.

The use of artificial nesting structures has a long history in wildlife management. In North America, nest boxes have had a positive impact on wood ducks. "Woodies" were decimated from overexploitation and loss of habitat throughout the latter half of the 1800s and the early 1900s. Such boxes undoubtedly aided the restoration of the species (Linduska 1987). Nesting baskets for mallards have even a longer history in Europe where they have been used for over 300 years (Henderson 1984). More recently, attention has been given to providing nesting boxes to a wide variety of cavity-nesting birds, from the small house wren and chickadee to the large barn owl. Such structures are especially valuable where natural cavities in dead trees and snags have been lost through intense forest management.

Other birds may respond to nesting structures, too. The mourning dove, American robin, great horned owl, Canada goose, osprey, bald eagle, golden eagle, and several hawks will use nesting platforms that are properly designed and located in appropriate habitat. Nesting platforms have facilitated management of a particularly troublesome situation in the western United States where many eagles and other raptors nest on power-line poles and towers. This activity can result in electrocution of birds, impacting the raptor population and disrupting the supply of electricity to people, as such electrocutions may cause power outages. Properly constructed and located nesting platforms on the power-line poles and towers allow the birds to nest safely.

The use of nesting structures as a management tool also has application in urban areas, particularly where natural habitat has been destroyed or highly modified. Before employing this management tool, a number of considerations must be addressed (Boone 1979, Yoakum et al. 1980, Robinson and Bolen 1989). Of overall importance is meeting the biological needs of the species under management. Nest boxes should be designed and constructed to proper dimensions, placed in appropriate habitat, erected at the proper height above ground, and maintained properly from year to year to assure continued use. In addition, boxes should be durable, predator-proof, weathertight, lightweight, and economical to build. By adhering to these guidelines, artificial nesting structures can substitute for a deficiency of natural sites in otherwise suitable habitat in urban areas for a wide diversity of species.

Many of the same species that use nesting structures in the countryside also will use the structures in town. The wood duck is one such species. Several wood duck boxes were erected on a residential lot of about 2.5 acres (one hectare) in Burlington, Iowa, in 1943 (more boxes were added later). As of 1988, some 6,000 ducklings had been produced. Hatching success in Burlington averages more than 80%, whereas the average success rate in the wild is less than 50% (Leopold 1951 and 1966 as cited in Hawkins et al. 1990). Such boxes are of most value to wood duck populations when (1) suitable breeding habitat is present but nesting cavities are absent or scarce, (2) nesting boxes are protected from predators, (3) new habitats are developed in areas with few cavities, and (4) competition for nest cavities is high (Hawkins et al. 1990). I believe these considerations apply to other species as well.

Chapter 8
Managing Urban Habitats for Wildlife

Nature of Urban Habitats

Urban habitats vary from densely built cores downtown to suburbs with large yards and considerable open space. In comparison with the rural countryside, however, urban habitats are relatively small patches of land. Most of the ground surface has been disturbed. Even so, many cities still retain remnants of natural habitat, sometimes well encompassed by concrete, but most often located nearer the urban–rural fringe zone. Such sites frequently are preserved as city or county parks, nature centers, or natural areas and provide tremendous recreational and educational opportunities. If managed properly, these lands also offer the best opportunity for maintaining native plants and animals of the region.

There are other habitats in the city. Business parks and industrial parks contain landscaped grounds and sometimes larger open space areas, such as wetlands and steep slopes, where development is restricted or prohibited. Institutions such as schools, hospitals, and churches (including cemeteries) occupy considerable land area and can be landscaped for people and wildlife. Neighborhood and community open spaces (and vacant lots) represent important urban habitats. Many such areas buffer streams, lakes, ponds, and wetlands from development. Backyards of individual residences offer habitat potential if managed with an eye toward wildlife. Running throughout the metropolitan environment are roads and railways that can

97

serve as corridor links between urban habitat and the countryside. All of these areas provide opportunities to consider wildlife in management schemes. They offer occasion for people to interact with nature and to get away from the hustle and bustle and stress of city life, if only for brief times.

Nature of Management

Managing the habitats of wildlife is the most important and most basic approach to wildlife management. This activity involves manipulating food, cover, water, and space in proper amounts and distribution for species of interest. Although simple in concept, the task is often difficult in practice because little is known about the specific habitat requirements of most species. With regard to food and cover, however, management generally means manipulating succession and the compositional makeup of vegetation to achieve suitable vegetation structure and food plants. Species such as white-tailed deer, ruffed grouse, and cottontail rabbit prefer midsuccession stages and edge habitat. Others, such as the northern spotted owl and the hooded warbler, require large blocks of late-succession mature forests. Denuded sites can be revegetated with plants beneficial to wildlife.

Providing unpolluted drinking water in adequate quantity is necessary for most terrestrial species. This is not generally a problem in high-rainfall areas but in drier regions such as the southwestern United States, drinking water for terrestrial wildlife is scarce and more attention is given to this habitat component. Many aquatic and semiaquatic species are water dependent, such as ducks, geese, swans, and numerous marsh birds and shorebirds. Mammals such as muskrat, beaver, and mink also are included, along with amphibians, reptiles, invertebrates, and fish.

Because of their productivity and the diversity of wildlife supported, wetlands are the focus of considerable current emphasis. Over half of the original wetlands have been lost in the United States (Tiner 1984), and much present effort is underway to preserve, create, restore, and manage the remaining wetland habitats. Just as terrestrial plant communities go through succession, so too do aquatic communities. Wildlife managers attempt to control succession and to maintain it at a stage most desirable for wildlife. An interspersion of vegetation and open water is best, and desired results generally can be obtained through regulation of water levels.

Space is a critical component of wildlife habitat. Although food, cover, and water may be present in a given habitat, adequate space is essential for wildlife populations to survive. As with the other elements of habitat, space requirements differ for different species. For example, the wolverine, North America's largest terrestrial mustelid (sometimes called the "skunk bear"), is perhaps a true wilderness species. It may require a home range of some 25,000 acres to more than 100,000 acres (10,000 to more than 40,000 hectares). As you might expect, habitat suitable for wolverines has shrunk considerably with human settlement of North America. White-tailed deer, on the other hand, may coexist with certain levels of development. The home range for deer is on the order of 375 to 750 acres (150 to 300 hectares). Cottontails need less than 25 acres (10 hectares) and meadow voles and white-footed mice less than 2.5 acres (one hectare). Thus, smaller animals generally can occur in urban areas if adequate food, cover, and water are present.

The type and degree of habitat management in metropolitan areas depend on one's objectives and the characteristics of the habitat itself. Small pocket parks and corner plazas downtown generally must be managed intensively. At the other extreme, natural areas will receive little or no management.

Before implementing management practices, it is important to inventory the site of interest and assess its value to wildlife. A first step is to map the various habitats and record characteristics useful to wildlife. At what successional stage is the vegetation? What plant species are present? Do they provide food and cover to wildlife? What are the structural properties of the vegetation? If the area is woodland, is leaf litter present on the forest floor and is an understory of shrubs present beneath the tree canopy? How many snags are present for cavity-nesting species, and how are they distributed over the site? Is the site homogeneous, or does it consist of several distinct habitat types? In case of the latter, how are the types interspersed? Finally, it is essential to record the type of water present on site—stream, pond, lake, or wetland. In practice, managing urban habitats usually will involve one or more of the following approaches.

Hands-off Management

In some instances, the management goal may be to "let nature take its course." If this decision is made, plant communities will, through natural succession, slowly change over time until the climax vegetation type for the region is reached. An oak-hickory forest may develop in the eastern United States, beech-maple in the Midwest, and hemlock-fir-cedar in the Pacific Northwest. Unless disturbed by natural catastrophe such as fire or disease, or unless cut by humans, these vegetation types will perpetuate themselves.

In the United States, most of the climax vegetation types have been destroyed. There are few places in the East where "old growth" or ancient forests remain, and efforts to maintain some of the old growth forests in the Pacific Northwest are meeting stiff resistance. The value of these areas as wildlife habitat increases as they become rarer because once they are gone so are the animal communities they support. The value of habitat also usually increases with the length of time needed to establish the habitat. For these reasons, hands-off management most typically applies to climax vegetation types or to situations where natural forces are being encouraged and perhaps studied.

In the metropolitan environment, such management generally is most applicable to urban forest or park natural areas. However, strictly hands-off management may not protect a site. Too many deer may impact the area by heavily overbrowsing it, inhibiting plant regeneration. So, if the management objective is to maintain and perpetuate the plant community, the deer may have to be controlled through active management, partly because natural predators are no longer present. Likewise, so-called invasive exotic species may encroach on the site—plants such as kudzu, Japanese honeysuckle, and purple loosestrife. Insect or disease outbreaks may occur, also threatening the community. If these are not controlled through active management, the habitat of interest may be lost or seriously degraded.

In summary, simply protecting a site from human intrusion may not guarantee perpetuation of that site. Strictly hands-off management seldom is practical in urban areas because human influence is now so pervasive and the natural habitats we want to protect are so small. Thus, although such management may be the approach of

Wide expanses of closely mown lawn provide little habitat to wildlife. Metropolitan homeowners can do much to improve front and backyards by planting trees, shrubs, and other vegetation of value to wildlife. (Photo: Carrol Henderson, Minnesota Department of Natural Resources.)

choice, it may very well turn into minimum active management on an area struck by lightning, infested with gypsy moths, or threatened in some other way.

Advancing Succession

Wide expanses of open lawn, perhaps with scattered trees and shrubs, are typical in the postdevelopment landscape. Such areas have little value to wildlife. A few species, such as robins and starlings, will feed on earthworms and other invertebrates near the soil surface, but wildlife diversity is severely restricted. To enhance the habitat value of such areas, more advanced successional stages are needed. One could take a hands-off approach and let succession occur naturally. Simply not mowing would allow the process to evolve. But this approach is slow, and the vegetation that grows may not be what the manager wants. As an alternative, one could speed up succession by planting trees, shrubs, vines, and herbaceous vegetation. Before doing so, it is important to know what kind of wildlife will benefit from various successional stages and thus what stage of advancement is desired. Meadow habitat (an early successional stage) will be attractive to a wide variety of butterflies and to birds and mammals such as meadowlarks, field sparrows, bluebirds, meadow voles, and, near the brushy edges, cottontails. Advancement to mature forest (a late successional stage), however, will be needed for vireos, thrushes, squirrels, chipmunks, and other woodland species.

Planting for landscape aesthetics and wildlife can be done in cities, towns, villages, and suburbs. Because of generally low-quality soils, altered climate, and other factors, however, it is sometimes difficult to get plants to grow that are desired in the landscape. Some species, such as dandelions and tree of heaven, are well adapted to the harsh urban environment, and many such plants have wildlife value. But a broader diversity of vegetation often is of interest. Therefore, it is essential to know the physical characteristics of the soil and its nutrient content. With such knowledge, one can match suitable vegetation with existing soil or treat the soil with fertilizers and other amendments to match the requirements of desired plants. Local county extension service personnel can explain the proper procedure and locations for having soils tested.

Giving preference to native species in the landscape planting scheme will help to ensure survival of the native plants and their associated wildlife communities. Unfortunately, most urban landscaping in the past incorporated exotic plants, and these still dominate local nurseries, although interest in native plants is growing.

In a landscape planting scheme for wildlife, it is also important to consider vegetation structure, arrangement (pattern), and species composition. With regard to vegetation structure and arrangement, both vertical layering and horizontal pattern are critical factors. For horizontal pattern considerations, clumping of vegetation to maximize patch size, rather than planting in rows, is best for birds (DeGraaf 1987) and probably for other species as well. Connecting patches with corridors also is important.

Removing the shrub layer, ground vegetation, and leaf litter from forested areas destroys habitat for wood thrush and many other species dependent on these forest characteristics. (Photo: Carrol Henderson, Minnesota Department of Natural Resources.)

Creating various vertical layers of vegetation, from ground covers to low and tall shrubs to trees, is essential to sustain a diversity of species (MacArthur and MacArthur 1961, Karr and Roth 1971). A mowed grass carpet beneath a tree canopy with no shrub layer is devastating to ground- and shrub-nesting birds. The wood thrush is a highly desirable bird and will live in urban areas—if habitat conditions are right. The bird requires a dense tree canopy with a shrubby understory and leaf litter on the forest floor (Roth 1987). This woodland bird is a low nester and forages primarily in leaf litter for invertebrates.

With regard to species composition, it is desirable to plant trees, shrubs, and other vegetation of known food and cover value to wildlife. (Appendices A and B provide some help in this regard.) Moreover, consideration should be given to wildlife use through the different seasons. For example, mulberry, cherry, and elderberry are good native summer plants for songbirds. Trumpet vine, hollyhock, and phlox provide food for hummingbirds. Throughout the growing season, diverse plants such as pussy willow (in the spring), hollyhock, butterfly bush, and asters (in the fall) are important to butterflies. Also during fall, dogwood and mountain ash are excellent wildlife plants. Through winter, hawthorn, red cedar, sumac, and trees such as hickory and oak provide food in the form of nuts, acorns, and persistent fruits. Conifers such as cedar, pine, and hemlock provide important winter cover. Once the desired stage of succession is reached, management may be required to maintain it.

If managers recognize the limitations posed by development, succession can be advanced on a small scale even in metropolitan centers. A 2.5-acre (one-hectare) redevelopment project in downtown Baltimore, Maryland, was landscaped with a variety of shrubs of value to birds. Included were two species of rose, barberry, pyracantha, flowering quince, and autumn olive. Pigeons, starlings, and house sparrows declined from 94% of the bird community to 52% over the three-year study period. Birds that increased included mourning dove, mockingbird, cardinal, house finch, northern junco, and American crow (Franklin and Adams 1980).

Plant community advancement also can be practiced on urban and suburban residential lots. In 1979, a half-acre (0.2-hectare) lot and a one-acre (0.4-hectare) adjoining pasture in Cedar Rapids, Iowa, were mowed or grazed to maintain lawn. The only other plants present were several large white oaks, a few box elders and elms, and one or two locusts. After 1979, 70 different plant species attractive to wildlife were added, mostly in clumps to enhance their wildlife value. Large conifers planted for winter cover included white pine, red pine, and eastern hemlock. Deciduous trees for food, cover, and nest sites included black cherry, mulberry, black walnut, black oak, and sugar maple. To develop a shrub layer, highbush cranberry, elderberry, gray dogwood, blackberry, and raspberry were planted. For the ground layer, bluestem, coneflowers, strawberry, butterfly weed, asters, and goldenrods were encouraged. In addition, a small pond was built. Over the years, some 65 bird species have been observed using the area. Included have been seven species of woodpeckers, seven species of warblers, great horned owl, ring-necked pheasant, and scarlet tanager. Among the mammals have been gray squirrel, fox squirrel, white-tailed deer, red fox, raccoon, opossum, chipmunk, woodchuck, cottontail, and two species of bats. The property has been registered as an urban wildlife sanctuary by the National Institute for Urban Wildlife.

Setting Back Succession

"Arresting" succession is the most widely practiced management technique in the metropolitan environment. It generally involves some mechanical means of cutting grass or trees and shrubs, with use of herbicides also quite common. Controlled fires (also called prescribed burns) are used frequently in rural areas, but fire has limited use in the urban environment.

Mechanical lawn mowers are most popular for maintaining succession in the short-grass stage. However, weekly cutting of lawns throughout the growing season does not provide much food or cover for wildlife. A better approach to assist wildlife would be to reduce the extent of closely mown lawn. Doing so does not necessarily mean loss of openness. If an open (or savannalike) characteristic is desired, an area can be maintained as meadow habitat. Simply mowing once a year, or better yet, once every two or three years, will eliminate shrub and tree seedlings and maintain succession in a grass-forb meadow stage of much greater value to wildlife than a lawn mown weekly. To retain some meadow habitat at all times, an area managed in this fashion should not be cut completely at any given time. To do so would deplete valuable food and cover. A much better practice would be to mow half the area one year and the other half the following year. If a three-year cycle is used, mow one-third of the area in any given year. This technique will always leave some habitat for wildlife while keeping the area in a dynamic state of early succession. Mowing in late winter–early spring will provide overwinter cover for wildlife and is preferable to summer or fall mowing. Late spring mowing should be avoided as it will interfere with the breeding season of many wildlife species.

This mowing scheme is most applicable to larger open space areas managed by city or county park and recreation departments, or similar authorities, with equipment capable of cutting down small shrubs and trees that sprout between mowing cycles. Small property owners with light mowers might find a single annual mowing difficult and a two- or three-year cycle impossible. However, such owners can easily remove any unwanted shrub or tree sprouts by hand. Meadows maintained in such fashion not only provide better wildlife habitat, but also do not require the enormous quantities of pesticides and fertilizers needed to maintain artificial stands of manicured grass. Meadows also are economical to maintain. I believe their use could be expanded in the metropolitan environment, but I do not advocate eliminating all formalized landscaping.

Another method of holding back succession that is applicable to urban areas is the cutting of woody growth with a power saw, handsaw, or ax. Normally, in most urban areas of North America, this will involve selective tree and shrub removal. Removing the overstory vegetation allows more light to penetrate to lower levels, resulting in more vigorous growth of herbaceous vegetation and lower shrubs. Depending on the manager's objective, trees alone may be removed, in which case a shrub community may develop, or both trees and shrubs may be cut, in which case an herbaceous meadow will be perpetuated (as I have described).

Many rights-of-way of highways, railways, pipelines, power lines, and underground cables offer opportunities for managing meadow or shrub communities. Past management of most rights-of-way consisted largely of maintaining grass cover by regular mowing throughout the growing season. Although, for good reason, trees cannot be allowed to grow on many of these areas, there are alternatives to frequent grass mowing. One good alternative is to maintain succession in a shrubland stage. Research has shown that such communities are relatively stable and can be maintained for long periods of time with minimal management, which generally consists of selective herbicide spraying of individual trees in early growing stages. Shrubs useful in this regard that also have good wildlife value include huckleberry, greenbrier, blueberry, speckled alder, gray dogwood, and nannyberry (Niering and Goodwin 1974).

There are now many examples of cooperative efforts between power companies, highway departments, and government and private conservation groups in managing rights-of-way with greater consideration to wildlife. One good example is Patuxent Wildlife Research Center, near Laurel, Maryland. In 1960, the U.S. Fish and Wildlife Service (which operates the research center) and Potomac Electric Power Company agreed to implement a management program that would develop a shrubland community on a newly con-

structed right-of-way on the property. Mowing was halted and selective applications of herbicide were periodically applied to stems of
unwanted species. After 30 years, the right-of-way was dominated
by a shrub community rich in botanical diversity and heavily used by
wildlife (Obrecht et al. 1991). Success of the program has led to
greater use of the technique by the power company.

Fire is frequently used in rural areas to set back succession, but its
use in the urban environment generally is not practical and often is
illegal. Risk of property destruction is great in the urban complex,
and smoke from fire adds to air pollution. Natural lightning fires occasionally do sweep through residential communities of southern
California, sometimes causing great economic loss. Ironically, small
periodic fires historically kept the fuel supply in check, lessening the
probability of a major conflagration. With the suppression of all fires
today, however, the fuel supply builds up and the potential for large-
scale destruction of property is increased.

Other forces that set back succession include insects and disease,
but I am unaware of either's being used purposefully for management. Their occurrence does, however, present another management
question: Should chemical sprays be used in an effort to control insects and disease? Managers must weigh this question carefully, considering the potential benefits of spraying in controlling the target organism, the impact of spraying on other species (including food
chain effects and hazards to humans), the likelihood of contaminating
surface and ground water supplies, and the possible alternatives such
as "integrated pest management." Integrated pest management is a
biological control approach to pest management that relies on para-
sites, predators, and pathogens, in addition to selective pesticides, to
maintain lower densities of an unwanted species.

Managing Edges

Habitat edge was defined earlier as the interface between two or
more structural types of vegetation. Urban areas have a lot of edge
habitat. Edges demark private property boundaries, occur along
streams, power lines, and transportation corridors, and are found in
cemeteries, on golf courses, and in community and neighborhood
parks where they separate active-use areas from passive-use areas.

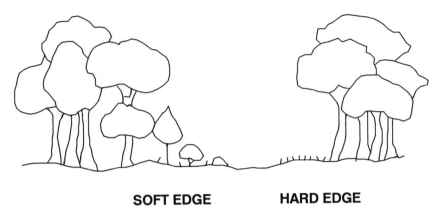

SOFT EDGE   HARD EDGE

Figure 9. Soft edges between meadow and woodland provide better wildlife habitat than do hard edges. There are many opportunities in the metropolitan environment to create soft edges.

Edges can serve multiple purposes. For people who find fences along property boundaries unsightly, "living fences" of trees or shrubs with wildlife value can be substituted that are aesthetically pleasing as well as functional for screening and privacy. A dense planting of hawthorn will be impenetrable to people, but will provide food and cover for wildlife. Combining taller trees and shrubs as background with shorter ones in the foreground also is aesthetically more pleasing and provides better habitat for wildlife. Such a design creates soft edge rather than hard edge (Fig. 9).

The open nature and numerous edges of urban areas offer good opportunity to manage habitat for butterflies. Such an objective is of value because past habitat destruction and widespread use of pesticides have decreased many butterfly populations. Also, meadows and soft edges are early successional stages and thus can be created in a relatively short period of time.

In establishing vegetation for butterflies in meadows and along edges, it is important to remember that butterflies need sun and protection from the wind. To be of most value, the habitat must provide food plants for both larvae and adult butterflies throughout the growing season from spring to fall. From a management standpoint, selection of perennials that will bloom successively from spring to fall will minimize management requirements (Mitchell 1986). Also, it is useful to visualize three different levels of vegetation and to select plants valuable to butterflies for each level (Booth and Allen 1990). Background vegetation is the tallest and may consist of a forested edge along a property boundary. If a wall or fence demarks the property boundary, background vegetation will need to be planted. Pussy willow blooms in early spring and is attractive to adults of such butterfly species as mourning cloak, comma, and question mark. Other early-blooming trees attractive to adults include plum, peach, and cherry. Trees representing good food sources for larvae include dogwood, spicebush, and various fruit trees. Caterpillars of the tiger swallowtail prefer to feed on leaves of the tulip tree, wild cherry, and white ash. American elm is attractive to the mourning cloak, question mark, and comma, and the silver-spotted skipper shows preference to black locust.

Attractive low shrubs should be planted in front of the taller background trees or woody vegetation. In late spring, shrubs such as lilacs attract swallowtails and monarchs. Throughout summer and into fall, smooth sumac, dwarf sumac, sweet pepperbush and butterfly bush are excellent selections. Shrubs supporting larvae include abelia, butterfly bush, and wax-leaf privet. In open woods, an understory of spicebush, sassafras, papaw, shadbush, and flowering dogwood is desirable.

Plant herbaceous vegetation in front of the shrubs. In early summer, butterfly weed is particularly attractive to adult fritillaries. Throughout the summer and into fall, phlox, fernleaf yarrow, black-eyed Susans, Saint-John's-wort, impatiens, marigolds, and asters are excellent nectar-producing plants for adults. Larval fritillaries feed on violets. Other good herbaceous food plants for caterpillars include milkweed and asters.

Although this discussion specifically concerns butterflies, the principles are sound for other kinds of wildlife as well. Meadow habitat and soft edges as substitutes for grass lawn and hard edges will benefit mammals such as meadow voles and cottontails and birds such as meadowlarks, field sparrows, and bluebirds. Planting edges that follow a curvilinear pattern present a more natural appearance that generally is more aesthetically pleasing than the effect created by straight edges.

Managing Water

Water is a vital natural resource. Not only is it required for wildlife, but it is necessary for human life as well. It is probably fair to say that we are still not managing water wisely. For example, many aquifers continue to be depleted and not to be adequately recharged. Numerous bodies of water are still considered by too many individuals as common dumping grounds for various by-products of present-day society. In financial terminology, water might best be considered a capital asset, and everyone knows that it is not wise to continue depleting your capital. Yet that is what we have done in the past with respect to water, and to a lesser extent are continuing to do today.

How can better management reduce these negative environmental effects and provide greater benefit to wildlife? To the extent possible, an overall management goal should be to maintain the hydrology of the area as it was before development. The first step toward this goal should be to start with better protection of water resources as development occurs. Valuable habitats should be identified, and protective measures implemented early on. Building should not occur in flood plains. These areas are important for maintaining local hydrology and provide valuable riparian habitat to wildlife. They also can be used in the postdevelopment landscape as recreational open spaces — and marketed as community assets (Reaume 1986). Thus, retaining vegetated buffer strips along streams and wetlands will help to maintain the functional integrity of these aquatic systems, including maintenance of wildlife communities.

Placement of fabric fences around construction sites and straw or hay bales in small drainages can help to minimize erosion during construction. Temporary sediment ponds can be used to detain water runoff, thus allowing time for much of the sediment to settle out. Permanent storm-water control impoundments also are effective in reducing sedimentation downstream and in controlling the flow of water from construction sites. Increased use of porous pavement and other means of increasing water infiltration in the postdevelopment landscape also will help.

Aquatic habitats already degraded by urbanization require more intensive management. With regard to streams, many of the techniques mentioned for maintaining stream integrity in the face of development also will assist in restoring degraded ones. Planting trees, shrubs, and other vegetation along a stream will help to buffer the impact of urbanization.

Restoring an urban stream may start with identifying any pollution sources contributing to its degradation and with taking corrective action to eliminate or reduce such pollution. Simply removing trash and debris also may be an early requirement. In addition, removing accumulated sediment from sections with large depositions and replacing that sediment with gravel beds will enhance fish habitat by providing spawning sites.

Where erosion of the stream bank is severe, riprap, gabions, or "root wads" may be needed. Riprap refers to large broken stones loosely placed along the stream bank to reduce or eliminate the erosive power of water. Gabions are wire cages filled with stones that may be used for the same purpose. Root wads, too, function to reduce stream bank erosion, but are somewhat more "natural appearing" than riprap or gabions. They are currently being used in reconstruction of streambeds and essentially are uprooted trees from which the tree crowns have been removed. The trunk and attached "root wad" are placed perpendicular to the flow of water, and earth is placed over the trunk, with the root wad thus providing support to the stream bank. Several root wads may be placed together along a stream.

Other techniques may be effective in restoring stream habitat. Small dams called check dams, perhaps no more than a log across the stream, sometimes are used to reduce water velocity and its erosive capabilities. Care must be taken in the design and construction of such dams to ensure that migratory fish can continue to use the stream unimpeded by the dam. Artificial riffles and pools may be constructed, if lacking in the stream. Stone boulders can be used to create riffles that help to oxygenate the water. Quiet, deeper pools provide cool retreats for fish. Restoring degraded streams is expensive. It is far better to protect such habitat as development expands than to institute corrective measures at a later date.

Many degraded wetlands also can be restored, and new ones created (Adams et al. 1986, Demgen 1988, Morrison and Williams 1988, and Zentner 1988). Excessive sediment deposited with the progression of development can be removed. If, through neglect, vegetation is too rampant, management practices can be instituted to benefit wildlife. The guidelines that follow can serve both for wetland res-

Streams often are heavily impacted by urbanization. A common scene in the metropolitan environment is stream bank erosion. Following rains, excess water from rooftops, parking lots, and streets is diverted to nearby stream channels. Thus, even small rainstorms can create flood conditions, and the high volume and velocity of water can erode the stream bank. (Photo: L. W. Adams.)

toration and for wetland creation in the metropolitan landscape. If the hydrology is too severely altered during development, however, what previously was a well-functioning wetland providing excellent

Gabions (wire cages containing stones) sometimes are used to protect urban
stream banks from erosion. (Photo L. W. Adams.)

wildlife habitat may never be fully restored in the postdevelopment
landscape.

Shallow water wetlands developed in association with the construction of storm-water control impoundments, gravel quarries,
and sewage treatment lagoons can, with a little consideration, provide wildlife habitat. To be of greatest value as wetland habitat, impoundments should be constructed with irregular shorelines, gently
sloping sides, and islands if the impoundment is larger than about
five acres (two hectares). Irregular shorelines increase the amount of
edge habitat and provide numerous nooks and crannies for waterfowl and other species. Among other things, this reduces the sight
line of breeding ducks and thus decreases territorial fights among
males. Irregular shorelines also help to reduce wave action at the
shore-water boundary, reducing erosion and encouraging vegetation
establishment.

Gently sloping sides, on the order of ten to one, will provide a lit-
toral shelf, or bench, of shallow water habitat around the impoundment. About 25% to 50% of the water surface area should be two

Ponds in the metropolitan landscape provide aesthetic and recreational values to people and habitat to wildlife. Such structures can help to better manage water resources in the urban environment. (Photo: L. W. Adams.)

feet (0.6 meter) deep or less. This will encourage wetland plant growth and improve resting and feeding habitat for dabbling ducks and a variety of marsh birds and shorebirds (Fig. 10). If mosquitoes are of concern, perhaps fish that feed on mosquito larvae and pupae, such as bluegill or mosquito fish, could be introduced. Bluegill are native to eastern North America and mosquito fish to the southeastern United States, but both species have been introduced widely elsewhere. Even so, careful evaluation should precede their introduction to avoid negative impacts on native species.

In larger impoundments, islands with gently sloping sides and appropriate vegetation provide nesting and resting sites for waterfowl and other wildlife. They also reduce nest predation by mammals. If permanent earthen islands are not possible, constructed floating ones are useful.

The kind, amount, and distribution of plants are important considerations. On the one hand, various species of pondweed, bulrush,

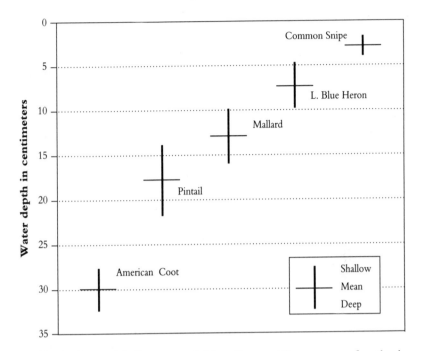

Figure 10. Bird use of shallow water habitat. By providing a range of wetland conditions, one can attract a diversity of wildlife species. (Source: Fredrickson and Taylor 1982.)

and smartweed provide excellent food and cover for waterfowl and other species. On the other hand, solid stands of cattail or common reed are of lesser value. As a general rule, maintaining an interspersion of open water and emergent vegetation in a ratio of about 50 to 50 is most ideal (Weller 1987). Also, emergent vegetation around the edge of the impoundment should not exceed 50% of the shoreline. Ducks, geese, and other species prefer such interspersion patterns.

Generally, seeding or planting is not necessary for vegetation establishment. Natural seed banks are usually adequate if water levels can be manipulated to induce germination (Weller 1987). However, if rapid plant establishment is required, transplants or sprouts can be used or the area can be seeded. On larger areas, particularly, wave action may inhibit natural vegetation establishment (Demgen 1988).

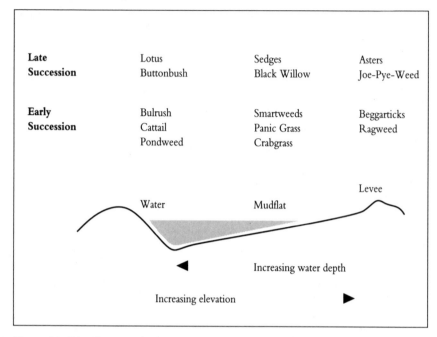

Figure 11. Distribution of selected moist-soil plants along a flooding gradient. Water level manipulation can assist in controlling succession and maintaining the right interspersion of vegetation and plant species composition. Such management benefits a diversity of wildlife. (Source: Fredrickson and Taylor 1982.)

In urban areas where the soil has been highly disturbed, it may be necessary to import marsh soil to ensure a source of seeds and rootstocks (Zentner 1988).

The capability of regulating water levels is a valuable tool for managing vegetation. The amount of standing water and the amount of soil moisture greatly influence plant species establishment and successional trends. Thus, water level regulation can assist in controlling succession and maintaining the right interspersion of vegetation and plant species composition. At greater water depths, early succession species such as bulrush, cattail, and pondweed will, over time, give way to lotus and buttonbush. On slightly drier sites, crabgrass, panic grass, and smartweed will yield to sedges and black willow. On drier sites still, beggarticks and ragweed will be replaced by asters (Fig. 11).

Drawdown refers to periodic removal of water from a wetland or water impoundment. It may be partial or complete. Maintaining a series of wetland sites in various stages of drawdown is best. Such moist-soil vegetation management is receiving considerable attention by wetland biologists. It is a sophisticated management technique as plant communities are dynamic and ever changing, and new knowledge continues to be gained. We do know that such management benefits a diversity of waterfowl, songbirds, shorebirds, marsh birds, mammals, amphibians, and reptiles.

As a final consideration for constructed impoundments, such facilities should be located near existing wetlands whenever possible. This will enhance their wetland wildlife value and ensure a seed source for vegetation establishment.

Better management of water will require public support. Public education programs can help to remind local citizens not to dispose of used motor oil, antifreeze, household cleaners, paints, solvents, pesticides, or other chemicals down household or storm drains. Such programs also are helpful for presenting guidelines for lawn and garden fertilization. For example, fertilizing after spring rains and not fertilizing to the water's edge will result in less nutrient flow into waterways and fewer adverse effects on the aquatic community.

Managing Human Activity

An important element of managing urban wildlife habitats is managing human activity in those habitats. This is particularly true for public open space areas and urban parks. Unlike in rural areas, in the metropolitan environment hunting generally is not allowed and management of that activity is not a significant concern, but other factors must be considered and evaluated. One such factor is human theft of vegetation. In a small nature reserve in Florida, six of 17 orchid species were extirpated due to robbery by humans (Dawson 1991).

Another factor not to be overlooked is significant disruption of the behavior and activity of animals. Some evidence indicates that intense human recreational use of forested areas reduces the density and diversity of breeding birds (van der Zande et al. 1984). This may be particularly true for ground and low-shrub nesters. Disturbance of breeding activity may result from the simple presence of large numbers of people in an area, or it may be more direct. Destruction of bird nests by children has been noted in some instances (Burr and Jones 1968).

Other potential impacts of humans should be considered. Heavy human use of an area may trample vegetation and compact the soil, leading to loss of plants and soil erosion. Particularly during dry conditions, discarded cigarettes and children playing with matches may increase the potential for accidental fire. People also may introduce undesirable exotic plants and animals to an area.

Although humans may indeed negatively impact urban wildlife habitats, urban parks and open space areas (and also state and national parks) are designed primarily for people. The public should be encouraged to use and enjoy such areas. This, however, does not mean that wildlife should be neglected. Part of a park's attraction to people is the wildlife it supports. The real issue then is how to balance human use of such areas with the needs of wildlife. An appropriate balance can only be achieved through effective management. An excellent example of such an approach is the natural resources management program recently established in Montgomery County, Maryland (Hench et al. 1987). In this suburban county adjoining Washington, D.C., at least 66% of each regional park (a park of at least 200 acres [81 hectares]) is to be maintained as natural or conservation areas. The remaining 33% may be developed for recreational activities (active-use areas). Natural areas enhance active-use areas by contributing to the character of the latter, by serving as outdoor classrooms for nature study and as outdoor laboratories for scientific research, and by providing the tranquil environment that many park users seek. Carefully designed trails—including those for walking, jogging, and horseback riding—can penetrate the nature conservation areas. Wildlife observation platforms, study blinds, food and cover plots, and feeding stations can facilitate a safe and enjoyable interaction between people and wildlife. In turn, active-use areas can positively impact nature conservation areas by providing a broad constituency of park users who can be called on to politically support the agency managing the park when alternative land-use proposals threaten a park's integrity.

There are other ways of minimizing detrimental impact on wildlife while providing human use and enjoyment. An on-site naturalist or warden has proven effective in reducing vandalism and other misuse by people. If a full-time position is not possible, regular inspection will help. Maintaining a certain degree of use by the public also will help to reduce misuse by a few individuals. During the breeding season, restrictions on human access may be necessary in certain areas. Finally, continuing public education is important. This can be through on-site signs, brochures, and programs and through the print, radio, and television media, as well as formally through local school systems. Only through such an approach can park managers meet the needs and desires of people while maintaining a responsibility to the wildlife resource, too.

Chapter 9

Managing Animals That Become Pests

Either knowingly or unknowingly, humans sometimes create exceptional habitat conditions for certain wildlife species in cities and suburbs. In previous chapters, I discussed general characteristics of these species as well as characteristics of populations that cause conflicts with society. The present chapter focuses on ways of managing these animals. It is not my intent to provide a comprehensive procedural guide to solving all pest problems. Rather, I highlight the different types of problems and outline a general approach to management, with some specific examples for illustration. Emphasis is placed on understanding and manipulating various habitat components. Usually it is an overabundance of one component or more—food, cover, water, or space—that creates a pest problem.

Animals That Enter Houses

Most terrestrial wildlife species seek shelter for protection from the weather and predators, and in which to raise their young. In doing so, they sometimes enter houses and other buildings designed for human use. Such occupancy may result in general annoyance or nuisance, or it may involve more serious property damage or threat to human health and safety.

Raccoons and squirrels are among the most common nuisance mammals in North America (de Almeida 1987). Bats, mice, and birds such as house sparrows, starlings, and pigeons frequently become pests by entering people's homes and other buildings. A biologist in Maryland who helps residents solve pest problems found that 90% of his calls deal with gray squirrels, birds, snakes, and bats (W. Bridgeland personal communication 1992). Attics, chimneys, garages, and basements are commonly targeted for occupancy by these critters. In addition, starlings and house sparrows may enter houses through unboxed eaves and unscreened louvered vents of clothes dryers or kitchen exhaust fans.

Most people who are aware of such occupation want the intruding animal or animals removed, and this is generally the wisest choice of action. Squirrels may chew insulation from electrical wires, creating a safety hazard. Bats and roosting birds potentially could transmit histoplasmosis, a respiratory disease caused by a microorganism living in accumulated bat or bird droppings. Raccoons, bats, skunks, and other animals may carry rabies viruses. Mice, raccoons, and other mammals may serve as hosts to the deer tick, which carries the organism causing Lyme disease. Pigeons reportedly can transmit more than 30 diseases to humans and another ten to domestic animals (Weber 1979). These are all good reasons for keeping wild animals wild, and for not attempting to make pets of them and for not allowing them to establish nest or den sites in our homes.

Human dwellings should be inspected periodically for evidence of wildlife intrusion. Attic, clothes dryer, and kitchen exhaust fan vents should be intact and screened. Animals gaining access to a building generally will discolor the paint or other finish around the entrance hole, leaving a dull or well-worn appearance; entry points are common at the juncture of the roof and sides. The inside of attics occasionally should be inspected for signs of wildlife use. The presence of mice, rat, bat, or bird droppings, nest sites, or chewed wires or wood is evidence of such use. If chimneys are not capped or screened, the inside should be inspected with a flashlight for possible use by raccoons or other animals.

If bats or birds have been roosting in an attic, expert advice should be sought before attempting to clean out accumulated droppings. Wild animals, including young ones, that seem tame or perhaps injured should not be handled; such animals may be diseased. The public health department or other experts should be contacted for assistance with both situations. Generally, by following these sensible precautions, and other ones mentioned throughout this chapter,

House chimneys sometimes provide secure den sites for raccoons in the metropolitan landscape. To prevent such occurrences, a cap can be placed on the chimney, allowing smoke to escape but preventing entry by raccoons or other animals. (Photo: D. A. Manski, National Park Service.)

there is little likelihood of humans contracting disease from wild animals. By keeping wild animals wild and free, we can continue to enjoy their presence around our homes.

Homeowners with wildlife intruders generally want the offending animal removed unharmed and released some distance away so that it will not return. Consequently, many animals are live-trapped and transported to more secluded habitat outside the city. However, this approach is not always a sound one. Mortality of transposed wildlife is frequently high, particularly if the new habitat already contains the species. Newcomers tend to travel more in search of unoccupied territory in which to live and reproduce. Road crossings are more frequent, and many animals are killed from collisions with vehicles. Diseases can be spread to new areas by transported animals, too. In much of the eastern United States, urban raccoons can no longer be live-captured and moved to the countryside. Rabies is now endemic in the population, and such movement would increase the potential for spread of the disease. Finally, removal of live-trapped animals from a given locality creates a vacuum that is simply filled by animals moving in from the surrounding area.

To avoid the various problems associated with live capture and translocation of wildlife, many biologists now recommend simply excluding the offending animal from a house or other building and repairing the access hole or capping the chimney so that reentry is prevented. Trained specialists use one-way doors that allow animals in the dwelling to leave but not reenter (Greenhall 1982, Hodge 1990). Once animals are excluded, entry holes are repaired. Cracks and crevices are boarded, caulked, or otherwise weatherstripped. Clothes dryers and kitchen exhaust fan vents are covered with heavy screen or hardware cloth if necessary, and chimneys are capped or screened. Such effort not only will prevent reentry by offending animals but also may improve the energy efficiency of the house. One-way doors should be used only when it is certain that young are not present in the building. Most animals have additional den sites in their territory and will continue to use them.

Burrowing Animals

Animals need not enter one's house to become pests. Skunks, opossums, woodchucks, and armadillos may create problems by denning under porches, decks, or concrete patios. Others such as moles, prairie dogs, pocket gophers, and ground squirrels may become a nuisance in the lawn. These animals are attracted to various habitat components in the metropolitan environment. Skunks and opossums are lured by garbage and pet food. Making such food sources unavailable will lessen the likelihood of these animals becoming pests.

By careful observation, one usually can determine the kind of animal using an underground den. Woodchucks are diurnal (active during the day) or crepuscular (active during twilight) and are fairly easy to observe entering or leaving their burrows or feeding nearby. They are generally shy animals and are unlikely to den too close to human activity. Skunks and opossums are mostly nocturnal (active at night), and direct observation of these mammals is less likely. However, a skunk den typically emits a characteristic odor, and black and white hairs often are present around the opening. If the occupant remains a mystery, the soil around the den can be loosened so that track impressions of animals entering or leaving the site will be noticeable. If the soil on site is unsuitable for track impressions, suitable soil can be imported or flour can be used.

Most animals can be evicted from underground dens with one-way doors. These are positioned over the den opening in such a way that an animal can exit but not return. This technique should not be used if it is suspected that young may be present in the burrow. Wait until the young are old enough to leave the burrow, and then install a one-way door. If the occupants are a mother skunk and her young, repeated filling of the hole with dirt may cause her to move her family to a new site (Hodge 1990). After all animals are removed, fill the hole with dirt or seal foundation openings with concrete, sheet metal, or wire mesh.

Norway rats also burrow under patios, decks, and along house foundations, but their burrows are noticeably smaller than those of woodchucks and skunks. Rats are attracted by unsecured garbage, pet food, spilled seed from bird feeders, and dog droppings. The most effective means of eliminating rats is to deny them such sources of food. This can be done with a little effort.

In the lawn, molehills above ground and mole tunnels just below the ground surface frequently are targets of human ire. However, moles are generally beneficial mammals. They eat harmful grubs and insects and aerate and mix the soil. Therefore, their presence should be evaluated carefully with these benefits in mind. Total elimination may not be desirable (or feasible). For small areas, repeated packing of runways by foot or roller may discourage use. Also for small areas, a sheet metal or hardware cloth fence may effectively exclude animals (San Julian et al. 1984, Hodge 1990). The fence should begin at ground level and extend downward 12 inches (30 centimeters) and outward from the area being protected at a 90-degree angle for 10 to 12 inches (25 to 30 centimeters).

Insecticides have been used to kill grubs and insects, thus reducing the food source of moles. However, these chemicals also are devastating to birds and other organisms in the environment. Of less detrimental impact to other life forms is milky spore disease, a natural control agent for certain white grubs, a major food source of moles (San Julian et al. 1984). This is a bacterial disease highly specific to the family of beetles to which the Japanese beetle belongs. Bacterial spores occur in the soil and are ingested by beetles as they feed. The disease does not affect earthworms, warm-blooded animals, or plants. If the disease is not present in a given area, milky spore can be purchased commercially for treating lawns, gardens, and similar areas. Also, commercial repellents containing thiram may protect flower bulb beds from mole damage (Henderson 1983, Hodge 1990).

Prairie dogs, pocket gophers, and ground squirrels are not easily excluded from areas by fencing, although such practice to exclude pocket gophers may be justified for valuable ornamental shrubs and trees (Case 1983, Hodge 1990). In this case, 1/4-inch to 1/2-inch (0.6- to 1.3-centimeter) hardware cloth should be placed to a depth of 18 to 20 inches (45 to 50 centimeters) below the surface of the ground. Ground squirrels prefer short-grass areas. If management options include allowing tall grass, ground squirrels will be discouraged from using the area. Legal rodenticides are the most effective means of control for these mammals, but such products should only be used by knowledgeable individuals (Boddicker 1983, Case 1983, Craven 1983c, Record 1983). Expert advice, assistance, and legal authority in the United States can be provided by the U.S. Cooperative Extension Service, the U.S. Fish and Wildlife Service, and the various state wildlife agencies. In Canada, similar support is available within the Canadian Wildlife Service and the provincial and territorial agencies.

Grazers in the Garden

Deer generally are the largest animals that cause widespread trouble by feeding in the garden and on landscape plantings around the home. Moose in Anchorage and other northern cities and elk in some localities occasionally may become a nuisance. Problems occur most often in suburbia and on the urban-rural fringe.

There are two native species of deer in North America, the white-tailed deer and the mule deer, with several subspecies for each. As pointed out in chapter 5, deer have been widely restored throughout North America and can reach high densities in metropolitan areas. Moreover, they are adaptable and have a broad diet.

Deer are browsers as well as grazers and are quite fond of many landscaping plants and garden vegetables. It is hard to find plants that they do not eat, although white-tailed deer have shown preference among common ornamental species (Conover and Kania 1988). They generally prefer broad-leafed evergreens over deciduous species and resinous evergreens such as pines, spruces, and firs. For example, during winter deer especially favor yews over American holly, shadbush, and flowering dogwood.

Controlling deer numbers in urban areas is not an easy task, although techniques are available to do so and may be classified as direct or indirect (Brush and Ehrenfeld 1991). Direct control methods include live capture and transfer, hunting, regulated sharpshooting, and reproductive inhibition. Indirect methods include repellents, fencing, and manipulation of succession and habitat interspersion.

Most often, urban residents experiencing a problem with deer want the animal or animals trapped unharmed and moved someplace else. This has been an effective technique for restoring populations in the past, but now it frequently is not a good option for handling urban deer problems. With widespread restoration of deer, it is difficult to find suitable habitat that is not already inhabited, and if deer are present in an area, they most likely are at carrying capacity for the habitat. New animals added to such areas have difficulty establishing home ranges, and mortality is higher than for resident deer (Jones and Witham 1990, Bryant and Ishmael 1991). Newly translocated deer travel more than the established resident deer and, in so doing, frequently are killed on highways. Translocated urban deer also have little fear of humans and experience higher mortality from hunting than do resident deer. Some animals die from capture-related stress. In addition, they sometimes become pests in the new area. Finally, live capture and translocation is expensive, with costs ranging from $273 to $400 per deer (Bryant and Ishmael 1991). So, unless suitable habitat is available that is devoid of deer, this technique is not a good option for handling nuisance urban animals.

Control techniques that inhibit reproduction also have public appeal, but methods tested to date are generally not yet perfected for use in management. Early work with steroids such as diethylstilbestrol (DES) and melengestrol acetate (MGA) showed that these drugs do inhibit reproduction in female deer, but the animals must be captured and the drug individually administered (see Brush and Ehrenfeld 1991 for a review). In addition, the drugs are carcinogenic and are passed through food chains. A promising new technique remotely delivers a vaccine that inhibits fertility by immunization. The procedure works experimentally and does not have the drawbacks of DES and MGA (Turner et al. 1992).

Hunting and regulated sharpshooting currently are the most effective direct techniques for controlling deer numbers, but these approaches are difficult to implement in metropolitan areas. Public opposition often is quite vocal, and safety is a major concern. Until 1975, urbanizing Princeton Township, New Jersey, had a shotgun season for deer. However, in that year, a no-firearm-discharge ordinance was passed. Over the following years, the deer population expanded, and browsing of ornamental landscape plantings increased as did deer damage to orchards. Increased deer mortality from collisions with vehicles on highways also was recorded. After review of alternative management approaches, the township returned to shotgun hunting in the fall of 1991.

An excessive deer population might be reduced through what is called a "welfare harvest." In this case, the meat is sent to a processing plant for later distribution to qualifying institutions and welfare agencies. Illinois has a Good Samaritan Food Donor Act that makes possible the processing of wildlife for welfare. The meat must be handled in a licensed facility and arrive at the welfare agency packaged. In 1986, white-tailed deer taken from suburban areas by sharpshooters were processed for such distribution. Also in 1986, deer taken by sharpshooters at the Minnesota Valley National Wildlife Refuge, in the St. Paul–Minneapolis metropolitan area, were donated to welfare agencies (Oetting 1987). Other states are initiating similar approaches.

Of the indirect methods for control of deer, fencing is the most effective, and several types have proven useful. Animals cannot jump over standard wire mesh fence that extends eight feet above the ground. However, such fencing is expensive. Various types of electric fencing are cheaper, but require more maintenance. Also, several designs of slanted or angled fence have been tested and found to be effective. In one design, posts are angled at 45 degrees, with the high end of the fence at least six feet above the ground. Wires may or may not be electrified. Deer walking under the angled fence are unable to jump it (Craven 1983b, San Julian et al. 1984, Hodge 1990).

Various repellents have been proposed for controlling deer damage, and some are commercially available. Commercial products such as Big Game Repellent and Hinder, along with human hair balls and products containing thiram, have shown variable effectiveness (Conover 1984). A dog tied to a long run or trained to remain in a designated area can effectively repel deer. Although I am unaware of any suitable tests, a so-called underground fence that restrains a dog within a given area may provide another option.

Finally, manipulation of plant succession and habitat interspersion may help to provide a long-term solution to excess deer. For white-tails in the East, reduction of habitat diversity and maintenance of late succession mature forest will lower an area's carrying capacity. However, habitat manipulation will most likely have to be combined with one or more other methods. Otherwise deer will overpopulate and overbrowse the site regardless of whether the carrying capacity is high or low.

Deciding on a method of deer control may not be an easy under-taking for a community. A facilitated approach whereby local repre-sentatives of a diversity of views are assembled into a task force can be effective in reaching final agreement. In this case, a professional facilitator conducts meetings and writes meeting summaries and final decisions made by the group. The task force must be charged with the responsibility to reach decisions on a timely basis for the citizens of the community (McAninch and Parker 1991).

Of the smaller animals, rabbits and woodchucks are among the most common species that can become pests in the garden. They can usually be excluded from such areas by fencing, and, unlike fencing for deer, fencing for these smaller animals is much less elaborate and expensive.

In the eastern United States, the eastern cottontail is the most abundant rabbit and most commonly involved in pest situations. It is easily excluded from small areas with 1-inch (2.5-centimeter) mesh poultry wire 18 to 24 inches (45 to 60 centimeters) high (Craven 1983a, San Julian et al. 1984, Hodge 1990). The bottom of the fence should be snug to the ground or buried a few inches. The fence may be temporary, if desired. It can be rolled up easily and stored for the next season.

During winter when food is scarce, rabbits will gnaw the bark from small trees and shrubs. Valuable landscape plants can be pro-tected from such destruction with handmade cylinders of 1/4-inch (0.6-centimeter) hardware cloth. These "small fences" should be constructed to extend at least 18 inches (45 centimeters) above the av-erage snow depth for the area in which they are used. In addition, they should encircle the tree or shrub several inches from the trunk or stem being protected. Stakes may be needed to securely hold the guard in place. Commercial tree wrap also can be purchased to protect valuable trees and shrubs.

In the western United States, blacktail jackrabbits and whitetail jackrabbits sometimes can become pests. Generally, the same methods can be used to exclude these species as are used for cottontails. However, larger mesh wire may be substituted, and it should extend higher above the ground because jackrabbits are larger than cottontails. Poultry wire with a 1 1/2-inch (3.8-centimeter) mesh size and extending 30 to 36 inches (76 to 91 centimeters) above the ground is effective (Knight 1983). For best results, the bottom six inches (15 centimeters) of the fence should be turned outward and buried six inches below ground level. With jackrabbits, as with cottontails, individual trees and shrubs can be protected with constructed woven-wire cylinders and commercial tree wrap.

Jackrabbits and cottontails also can be effectively trapped by knowledgeable individuals. However, trapping will only provide a temporary solution because the area will rapidly repopulate.

Woodchucks are good climbers and diggers, and a somewhat more sturdy fence is required for them than is needed for rabbits. A 2-inch by 4-inch (5-centimeter by 10-centimeter) mesh wire fence extending two to four feet (0.6 to 1.2 meters) above ground and one foot (0.3 meter) below ground is required for best results. The bottom six inches (15 centimeters) or so of the below ground portion should be turned outward. In addition, a single strand of electrified wire should be placed on top of the fence or placed four to five inches (10 to 12 centimeters) from the fence and the same height above the ground (Bollengier 1983, San Julian et al. 1984, Hodge 1990).

In various regions, localized wildlife problems appear. In Arizona, javelina (collared peccary) sometimes become pests by rooting in gardens and yards for food. In Florida and other southern states, armadillos cause similar problems by uprooting plants in search of insects and earthworms. Both species generally can be excluded from small areas by use of specialized fencing. Biologists of the agencies mentioned under the section "Burrowing Animals" are generally the best sources of information for wildlife matters of this nature.

Roosting Birds

Many species of birds, particularly migratory ones, form flocks in winter but disperse to individual breeding and nesting sites during summer. "Blackbirds" exhibit such behavior. In the southeastern United States where large winter roosts are common, blackbird flocks generally consist of several species, with red-winged blackbirds, starlings, common grackles, and brown-headed cowbirds being most typical. Winter flocks of blackbirds roost in large concentrations and typically reuse roosting sites nightly. Some roosts are in metropolitan areas. Large roosts, particularly, can cause damage or create nuisance problems. In some instances, the sheer weight of birds may break tree branches. However, it is the noise, foul odor, and unsightly mess of accumulated bird droppings on sidewalks, cars, and buildings that are most annoying to urban residents. The droppings are corrosive and can deface homes, buildings, and automobiles if not removed regularly. Accumulated droppings from roosts that are used repeatedly over several years create an environment for growth of the fungus that causes histoplasmosis in humans, a disease of the respiratory system. Histoplasmosis generally is not a problem unless the accumulated deposits of bird droppings are disturbed.

Two general nonlethal approaches to controlling or managing such roosts are habitat modification and scaring devices (Booth 1983, San Julian et al. 1984). Habitat modification usually has to be pretty drastic to be effective. Massive thinning of perhaps one-third to three-fourths of roost trees may be needed to move blackbirds to another roosting area. Such extensive alteration of habitat has major impact on other species, and people frequently do not wish to lose so many trees.

Scaring tactics most often used consist of various devices. Tape-recorded alarm and distress calls of birds can be played through loud speakers at roost sites, discouraging incoming birds from landing (Frings and Jumber 1954, Block 1966). Effectiveness of this method is enhanced by moving the playback calls throughout the roosting area. So-called "shell crackers" also can be effective. These typically are 12-gauge exploding shells fired from a shotgun. Explosions in the air near birds are more effective than those near the ground. Automatic LP gas exploders also should be elevated above the ground for best results, and effectiveness of these devices is enhanced by mobility. Generally, no single technique is effective when used alone. Experience has shown that it is better to integrate a combination of techniques into a scaring program (Johnson et al. 1985). Timing and other details are important. Typically, a scaring program should be started in the evening on arrival of the birds at the roost and continue until dark. The procedure is repeated for four to five nights, which is usually adequate to move the birds elsewhere. Moving blackbirds from large roosts requires professional help, and biologists of the agencies mentioned under "Burrowing Animals" in this chapter should be consulted.

In drastic cases, lethal methods have been employed for controlling blackbirds. PA-14, a wetting agent, is the only chemical registered with the U.S. Environmental Protection Agency for such control. The chemical functions as a detergent and is sprayed with water on roosting birds after dark on cold evenings. PA-14 strips the oil from the feathers of birds, thus destroying the feathers' insulative properties, and birds die from hypothermia (Stickley et al. 1986). Under suitable environmental conditions and proper technique, large numbers of birds will be killed. Surviving birds generally avoid the roost site for the remainder of the year and the subsequent winter, but the probability of birds using the site again for roosting increases over time (Glahn et al. 1991).

In addition to large blackbird roosts, urban residents sometimes have problems with smaller numbers of roosting or congregating house sparrows, starlings, and pigeons. These species will use various nooks, crannies, and ledges, both inside and outside buildings, and usually can be excluded from such areas by modifying the habitat (Courtsal 1983, Fitzwater 1983, Johnson and Glahn 1983, Hodge 1990). To exclude birds from indoor roosts, access ports can be closed with wire screen, plastic, or nylon netting or with metal, glass, wood, or masonry. The underside of rafters in airplane hangers, rail terminals, and similar structures can be covered with netting to prevent access by birds.

Outdoor ledges of buildings also can be modified to exclude these birds. Flat ledges can be angled at 45 degrees or greater with masonry, wood, sheet metal, or stone. Another technique that can be effective is use of "porcupine wires": Sharp, upright wires are attached to a ledge, making it difficult for birds to land and walk around. Available commercially are several sticky, nontoxic repellents that also can be placed on ledges to discourage bird use.

There are various other techniques, including chemical sterilants and toxic poisons, that may be effective in solving a roosting bird pest problem. Use of some of these products is restricted to certified applicators or persons under the supervision of certified applicators.

Aquatic Specialists

Water is an attractive feature for people in urban areas; lakes and ponds are particularly valued. Such areas also provide habitat to some distinctive wildlife species. As pointed out earlier, mallard ducks and Canada geese often find urban impoundments attractive, and sometimes populations increase to pest proportions. Fecal matter from too many birds may create messy sidewalks and lawns. In addition, bird droppings are an organic fertilizer and stimulate excessive algae growth in lakes and ponds. Geese, particularly, pose a hazard at airports when they frequent these areas for feeding on the abundant grass surrounding the runways. Mammals such as beaver and muskrat also may increase to undesired levels. Muskrats may damage earthern dams of ponds and lakes through construction of their burrows. Beavers, through their dam-building activity, may flood areas that people do not want flooded—including yards and basements of houses. They also may obstruct ditches and culverts, leading to periodic flooding during rainstorms. In addition, beavers sometimes cut down ornamental shrubs and trees of residential areas. When these problems arise, people want solutions, but they often do not want the animals harmed.

As with other pest situations, biologists do not have complete answers to aquatic pest problems. All too often, little research has been conducted on the usefulness of various proposed techniques. Progress, however, is being made slowly, and some help is available.

Live capture and translocation is perhaps the most publicly acceptable technique for dealing with excess ducks and geese, and it is effective if properly done (Adams et al. 1987, Cooper 1987, Oetting 1987, Cooper 1991). However, the procedure is labor intensive and expensive, and ultimately will be self-limiting as other areas establish populations. Geese are most effectively captured during an approximate three-week period in summer when they are growing new feathers and are thus flightless. During this time, the birds are easily "rounded up" in walk-in corral-type traps. Mallards, on the other hand, are most effectively captured on cold winter days in walk-in bait traps.

Another approach to controlling waterfowl is to employ scare tactics. Objects that move in the wind, such as scarecrows, tethered balloons, flags, and aluminum pie plates, sometimes can be effective. Black plastic flags may be the most useful and least expensive technique in this category. Flags can be constructed from three-mil-thick black plastic cut into two-foot by three-foot (0.6-meter by 0.9-meter) pieces and stapled to a four-foot (1.2-meter) wood lath (Pfeifer 1983, San Julian et al. 1984, and Hodge 1990). One flag per acre (two or three flags per hectare) should be placed in fields where waterfowl have been feeding and one per five acres (one per two hectares) in undamaged fields. The effectiveness of such tactics may be short-lived because birds usually learn quickly that no real danger is present.

Explosive scare devices also may move birds to other locations (Aguilera et al. 1991). Such devices include automatic propane exploders as well as so-called "screamer" shells, "shell crackers," and other manually operated noisemakers. Propane exploders should be set to fire about every ten to twenty minutes and should be elevated. They should be moved every two to three days so that birds do not become habituated to them. Manually operated explosive devices are most effective if directed through the air over birds.

A third approach to pest waterfowl situations is to create a barrier to the habitat or otherwise modify the habitat so that it is less attractive to birds. Unfortunately, features that make a lake or pond attractive to waterfowl often are those that are attractive to people too. At the extreme, impoundments can be dewatered, but this drastic measure is not likely to be publicly acceptable. Geese, particularly, like to walk from the water's edge to surrounding lawns and other grassy open spaces for grazing. In doing so, they seek an unobstructed view to remain vigilant toward predators. Birds may be discouraged from using a body of water by cessation of mowing to the water's edge in conjunction, perhaps, with planting of a shrub hedge or erection of a fence. Removal of islands and floating nest sites also can be effective in discouraging use (Oetting 1987).

Hunting or otherwise humanely reducing a population is a fourth approach to a pest problem. Hunting is not generally feasible in most urban situations. However, a goose or duck population might be reduced through a welfare harvest as discussed for deer in the section "Grazers in the Garden." In the present case, birds could be trapped and humanely killed, with the meat subsequently sent to a processing plant for later distribution to qualifying institutions and welfare agencies.

Last, if a problem situation exists and birds are being fed by people, such feeding should cease as other control measures are implemented. Supplemental feeding may be the primary reason for the concentration of birds, leading to the pest situation and contaminated water. Although popular with people, artificial feeding most likely does not benefit waterfowl populations. A better approach would be to enhance natural habitat features with a goal of maintaining birds at carrying capacity with the available habitat. A policy for supplemental winter feeding of waterfowl under emergency conditions, however, should be established by local jurisdictions, with assistance from appropriate federal, state, provincial, or territorial agencies. Because even such emergency feeding discourages the natural migratory behavior of waterfowl, the policy's detailed guidelines should include a clear definition of conditions when feeding is permissable, types of feed to use, and responsibilities for the program (Adams et al. 1987). Whichever approach, or combination of approaches, is implemented, urban waterfowl flocks might best be managed primarily by the jurisdiction where the birds are located, with strong public input and technical and planning assistance from federal and state, provincial, or territorial conservation agencies (Nelson and Oetting 1982, Adams et al. 1987).

Several approaches can be used to help alleviate problems caused by beavers in an urban setting (Miller 1983a, San Julian et al. 1984, and Hodge 1990). Fencing can be used to keep these mammals from small ponds, lakes, and valuable trees and shrubs. Individual trees and shrubs can be wrapped in hardware cloth, wire mesh, or tree wrap to a height of three and a half to four feet (1 to 1.2 meters) from the ground. In addition, several devices can be used either to lower pond water level or to keep it from rising. This may cause the animals to move elsewhere.

In the past, many nuisance beavers were live-captured and moved to new locations. This approach is still practiced today, but release sites lacking animals are less common. Furthermore, live capture and

Beaver populations are thriving throughout much of North America, including many urban areas. In low numbers, they usually can be accommodated in cities, towns, and villages and are appreciated by residents. Too many animals, however, may prompt complaints from citizens upset at the loss of backyard trees and shrubs, which are used as beaver food and construction material for dams and lodges. (Photo: L. W. Adams.)

translocation is a temporary solution in the problem area, as more beavers will immigrate from surrounding lands.

Beavers can be trapped effectively with kill traps. Such trapping is controversial, particularly in an urban setting. However, the city of London, Ontario, established legal agreement with the London Trappers Council to implement such an approach. The agreement provides city residents with nuisance wildlife removal services. As an incentive for handling nuisance animals year-round for an agreed-upon fee, the city allows members of the council to trap, during the regulated season, on designated lands owned or controlled by the city. Only trappers who have completed a special course in management and conservation and a special training session on urban trapping techniques can participate in the program (Williams and Mc-Kegg 1987).

Muskrats, too, can be controlled effectively by kill trapping. In addition, they may be excluded from burrowing into dams by use of riprap or mesh wire (Miller 1983b, San Julian et al. 1984, and Hodge 1990). A continuous layer of riprap two feet to three feet (0.6 to 0.9 meter) above and below the water level will discourage burrowing. Welded or galvanized mesh wire buried along the same area also will discourage burrowing. The wire, however, will eventually rust and disintegrate, and have to be replaced.

Reducing the water level of ponds and lakes at least two feet (0.6 meter) during winter will cause muskrats to move. Burrows can then be filled in, and the area riprapped with stone, or wire mesh can be installed (Miller 1983b). If work cannot wait until winter, one can probe with a rod above the burrow entrance to locate the nest chamber. Once located, the nest chamber can be exposed by removing the overlying earth. This procedure will cause muskrats to abandon the site, and adults will remove young. The burrow then can be filled in, and a barrier installed (Hodge 1990).

Other species sometimes can become a nuisance in urban areas. In the spring of 1983, I received a phone call from a townhouse resident in Columbia, Maryland, who was having difficulty sleeping at night. His insomnia was caused by a chorus of male bullfrogs attempting to attract mates in a small pond outside the bedroom window. Other residents experienced similar difficulty in sleeping. It turned out that the newly constructed pond was highly unbalanced and contained hundreds of bullfrogs (and even more tadpoles), but few predators of these amphibians. In an effort to create a more balanced system, largemouth bass fingerlings were stocked that summer. In addition, for some immediate relief, 140 adult bullfrogs were removed. The following year, 228 frogs were taken from the pond. In 1985, 73 frogs were removed and in 1986, 47 were taken. No frogs have been removed since that date. Over the years, the bass have grown and are now holding the frogs in check. One can still hear the deep-throated croak of a bullfrog on a late summer's evening, and most residents find that aesthetically pleasing. In this case, as in many other wildlife pest situations, it was the sheer number of animals that was objectionable.

Chapter 10
Looking to the Future

To the degree that we come to understand other organisms,
we will place a greater value on them, and on ourselves.
— Edward O. Wilson, *Biophilia*

People living in metropolitan areas enjoy wildlife. A recent survey estimated that 58% of Americans (16 years old and over) carried on an active interest in wildlife around the home through such activities as observing, identifying, photographing, and feeding wildlife, or through maintaining natural areas or plantings such as shrubs and other vegetation for benefit to wildlife. Furthermore, some 65% of the adult population enjoyed seeing or hearing wildlife while pursuing other activities, such as lawn care, around the home (U.S. Fish and Wildl. Serv. 1988). A comprehensive survey of Canadians reported similar results (Filion et al. 1983).

Urban Wildlife and Habitat Values

Why do people express such interest in wildlife? Of what value are wildlife and plants in one's daily life? These are difficult questions with no easy answers. There may be a deep-rooted need, grounded in millions of years of evolution, for humans to have animals nearby. Harvard University biologist Edward O. Wilson (1984) argued this point and coined a new word, "biophilia," that he defined as the human bond with other species. Perhaps Chief Seattle, an American Indian of the Duwamish and allied tribes of Puget Sound, Washington, realized this need many years earlier, in 1865, when he said, "If all the beasts were gone, man would die of great loneliness of spirit." In other words, humans have been an interdependent part of a living

Wildlife in the metropolitan landscape is enjoyed by people of all ages.
(Photo: Jay Anderson.)

system for millions of years. We have depended on plants and animals to sustain our own lives and perhaps have some innate need for these other life forms.

A "nature restoration hypothesis" has been proposed that incorporates the notion that natural views of trees and other plants tend to reduce human stress and anxiety (Ulrich 1979). There is some medical evidence that postsurgical recovery is faster for patients in rooms with a window view of a natural setting. In their urban landscapes, people prefer trees, especially, over other plantings, and neighborhood parks with a more informal, natural, and diverse landscape character are preferred over those with a less natural, more formal character (Gold 1986).

Doctors and allied medical professionals are recognizing the health benefits of companion animals—mostly cats and dogs to date, but perhaps the same can be said of wild animals when people enjoy them as wild animals. Research in the last decade has shown that animal association may contribute to higher first-year survival following coronary heart disease and to reduction in blood pressure, heart rate, and anxiety level in healthy individuals (Bustad 1987).

There are multiple sociological, educational, ecological, environmental quality, and scientific reasons for conserving wildlife and wildlife habitat in urban areas. Urban open spaces designed for people and wildlife provide places for human recreation and relaxation, and such areas offer tremendous opportunity for teaching young people about nature. Conservation of urban wildlife and habitat helps to maintain biological diversity—the numerous species of plants and animals found throughout the world—thus reducing the threat of species' becoming endangered and possibly extinct. In discussing the importance of maintaining biological diversity, Dennis Murphy (1988) pointed out that, "Our urban centers can be viewed as bellwethers of our global environmental fate. Our success at meeting the challenges of protecting biological diversity in urban areas is a good measure of our commitment to protect functioning ecosystems worldwide. If we cannot act as responsible stewards in our own backyards, the long-term prospects for biological diversity in the rest of this planet are grim indeed."

With regard to environmental quality values, trees and shrubs ameliorate high and low temperatures, reduce wind velocity, provide shade, and filter or block glare, all of which increase human comfort. Also, plants are useful in landscape architecture, erosion control, watershed protection, wastewater management, noise abatement, and air pollution control. These values are expressed in the marketplace, as trees increase the value of both developed and undeveloped land, and parks and open space add value to adjacent properties (see Smardon 1988 for a review).

Wildlife and habitat in urban areas also hold scientific value. In addition to our limited knowledge of the value of plants and animals for use in medicine, agriculture, and industry, there is much to be learned about the structure and function of ecosystems, both disturbed and undisturbed ones. Only from a sound knowledge base will we be able to manage wildlife and other natural resources effectively for their multiple benefits and values.

These are strong values even though it is often difficult to assign dollar amounts to them. There are other "values" to which it is even harder to assign a monetary figure. How do we place a dollar value

Wildlife adds an aesthetic dimension to the urban
landscape, and such value may be difficult to price.
(Photo: J.M. Hadidian, National Park Service.)

on the sound of songbirds on a spring morning, the flight of Canada
geese on a crisp autumn day, or the joy of watching a child pick wildflowers in a meadow? In our market economy, we may not be able to
place dollar amounts on these things, but I think most would agree
that they have worth. Thus, we should be cautious in disregarding
things we cannot immediately price. Aldo Leopold (1953) offered
sage advice many years ago when he wrote, "The last word in igno-
rance is the man who says of an animal or plant: 'What good is it?' If
the land mechanism as a whole is good, then every part is good,

whether we understand it or not. If the biota, in the course of aeons, has built something we like but do not understand, then who but a fool would discard seemingly useless parts? To keep every cog and wheel is the first precaution of intelligent tinkering."

International Urban Wildlife Efforts

Although this book has focused on North America, there is global work being conducted in urban ecology and urban wildlife conservation. The Man and the Biosphere Program of the United Nations Educational, Scientific, and Cultural Organization has, for many years, maintained an "urban ecosystems" component to study cities as ecological systems around the world. The British are highly successful in generating local public interest and support for urban nature conservation through volunteer urban wildlife groups. In addition, nature conservation schemes have been prepared for many municipalities. These schemes, or plans, are not statutory documents but nonetheless provide guidance to local authorities. In the Netherlands, a national plan has been formulated for establishing urban forests at the fringes of urban zones. A major goal is to concentrate development in a few existing cities and to integrate open space in the heartland. An academic unit at the Technical University of Berlin has extensive expertise in urban vegetation mapping. The Polish Academy of Sciences conducts research in urban ecology and has an impressive published literature on urban birds and other wildlife. Researchers in Japan are attempting to better understand urban ecosystems and urbanization processes and the effects of changed environments on humans.

All this work is only a sample of what is occurring around the world. I see no reason why it should not continue and expand in the future. I think there is growing recognition worldwide that human life is interconnected with the natural world and that we are dependent on it for our own survival and advancement. I am convinced that responsible environmental and resource protection and sustained economic development (human welfare) are mutually dependent, not mutually exclusive. As evidenced in many developing areas of the world, environmental protection and resource conservation receive low priority under struggling economies. However, sustained economic development is dependent on maintenance of clean air and water, unpolluted soil, and the many associated natural resources.

A Conservation Ethic

Noting the values of urban landscapes, many of which are difficult if not impossible to define economically, I believe we need to develop a strong conservation land ethic, first advocated by Aldo Leopold (1949) over 40 years ago. Leopold viewed land broadly as encompassing soil, water, plants, and animals, and pointed out:

> A land ethic of course cannot prevent the alteration, management, and use of these "resources," but it does affirm their right to continued existence, and, at least in spots, their continued existence in a natural state.
>
> In short, a land ethic changes the role of *Homo sapiens* from conqueror of the land-community to plain member and citizen of it. It implies respect for his fellow-members, and also respect for the community as such.

Leopold regarded a land ethic as a limitation on freedom of action, requiring human obligation. He felt that a major reason for the lack of a land ethic was that property was viewed only in economic terms, entailing privileges but not obligations. According to Leopold, "Obligations have no meaning without conscience, and the problem we face is the *extension of the social conscience from people to land.*" (Emphasis added.) To develop such a land ethic, we must think in terms of what is ethically and ecologically right as well as in terms of what is of immediate economic value. The interest shown in environmental matters from all segments of society in the recent 20-year anniversary celebration of Earth Day and the continued grassroots effort to sustain that interest leave me optimistic that society is moving toward Leopold's conservation ethic. I hope that is the case.

Appendix A

Landscaping for Wildlife (a selected bibliography)

Most of these publications are available through libraries, bookstores, garden centers, and seed and garden catalogs. A few are more difficult to find and can be obtained from the publisher or a particular source; for these, complete addresses for ordering are included in the listing.

Anderson, E. S., and A. P. Gillespie, eds. 1992. The National Wildflower Research Center's wildflower handbook: a resource for native plant landscapes. 2nd ed. Voyageur Press, Stillwater, Minnesota. 304 pp.

Baines, C. 1985. How to make a wildlife garden. Elm Tree Books/Hamish Hamilton Ltd., London, United Kingdom. 192 pp.

Baines, C., and J. Smart. 1991. A guide to habitat creation. rev. ed. Packard Publishing Ltd., Chichester, West Sussex, United Kingdom. 104 pp. Available from: London Ecology Unit, Bedford House, 125 Camden High St., London NW1 7JR, U.K.

Briggs, S. A., ed. 1973. Landscaping for birds. Audubon Naturalist Society of the Central Atlantic States, Inc., 8940 Jones Mill Rd., Chevy Chase, MD 20815. 62 pp.

Cerulean, S., C. Botha, and D. Legare. 1986. Planting a refuge for wildlife: how to create a backyard habitat for Florida's birds and beasts. Florida Game and Fresh Water Fish Commission, 620 S. Meridian St., Tallahassee, FL 32301. 33 pp.

Decker, D. J., and J. W. Kelley. n.d. Enhancement of wildlife habitat on private lands. Information Bull. 181. Cooperative Extension Service, Cornell University, Ithaca, NY 14853. 40 pp.

DeFazio, J. T. 1990. Developing backyard habitats in Mississippi. USDA Soil Conservation Service, 100 W. Capitol St., Suite 1321, Jackson, MS 39269. 20 pp.

DeGraaf, R. M., and G. M. Witman. 1979. Trees, shrubs, and vines for attracting birds. Univ. Massachusetts Press, Amherst. 194 pp.

Dennis, J. V. 1985. The wildlife gardener. Alfred A. Knopf, Inc., New York. 293 pp.

Diekelmann, J., and R. Schuster. 1983. Natural landscaping: designing with native plant communities. McGraw Hill Book Company, New York. 264 pp.

Dillon, O. W., Jr. 1975. Invite birds to your home: conservation plantings for the Southeast. Program Aid 1093. Soil Conserv. Serv., U.S. Dept. Agric., Washington, D.C. 16 pp.

Dove, L. E., T. M. Franklin, and L. W. Adams. 1985. "Plant" wildlife in your yard. Am. Forests 91:13-16.

du Pont, E. N. 1978. Landscaping with native plants in the Middle-Atlantic region. The Brandywine Conservancy, Inc., Chadds Ford, PA 19317. 72 pp.

Foote, L. E., and S. B. Jones, Jr. 1989. Native shrubs and woody vines of the southeast: landscape uses and identification. Timber Press, Beaverton, Oregon. 269 pp.

Geis, A. D. 1980. Relative attractiveness of different foods at wild bird feeders. Special Sci. Rep. — Wildl. No. 233. U.S. Fish and Wildl. Serv., Washington, D.C. 11 pp.

Gunnarson, L., and F. Haselsteiner, eds. 1990. Butterfly gardening: creating summer magic in your garden. Sierra Club Books, San Francisco, California and National Wildlife Federation, Washington, D.C. 192 pp.

Henderson, C. L. 1992. Woodworking for wildlife: homes for birds and mammals. 2nd ed. Minnesota Dept. Nat. Resour., St. Paul. 111 pp. Available from: Minnesota Bookstore, 117 University Ave., St. Paul, MN 55155.

Henderson, C. L. 1987. Landscaping for wildlife. Minnesota Dept. Nat. Resour., St. Paul. 145 pp. Available from: Minnesota Bookstore, 117 University Ave., St. Paul, MN 55155.

Hightshoe, G. L. 1987. Native trees, shrubs, and vines for urban and rural America: a planting design manual for environmental designers. Van Nostrand Reinhold, New York. 819 pp.

Leedy, D. L., and L. W. Adams. 1984. A guide to urban wildlife management. National Institute for Urban Wildlife, Columbia, MD 21044. 42 pp.

Marriage, L. D. 1975. Invite birds to your home: conservation plantings for the Northwest. Program Aid 1094. Soil Conserv. Serv., U.S. Dept. Agric., Washington, D.C. 20 pp.

Martin, A. C., H. S. Zim, and A. L. Nelson. [1951] 1961. American wildlife and plants. A guide to wildlife food habits. Dover Publ., Inc., New York. 500 pp.

Martin, L. C. 1990. The wildflower meadow book: a gardener's guide. 2nd ed. Globe Pequot Press, Old Saybrook, Connecticut. 320 pp.

McKinley, M. 1983. How to attract birds. Ortho Books, San Francisco, California. 96 pp.

Mirick, S., and N. Rennie. n.d. A planting guide for east Tennessee wildlife. Ijams Audubon Nature Center, 2915 Island Home Ave., Knoxville, TN 37920. 44 pp.

Mooberry, F. M., and J. H. Scott. 1980. Grow native shrubs in your garden. The Brandywine Conservancy, Chadds Ford, PA 19317. 68 pp.

National Wildlife Federation. 1974. Gardening with wildlife. Natl. Wildl. Fed., Washington, D.C. 190 pp.

Nokes, J. 1986. How to grow native plants of Texas and the Southwest. Texas Monthly Press, Inc., Austin. 404 pp.

Nordstrom, S. 1991. Creating landscapes for wildlife . . . a guide for back yards in Utah. Div. of Wildl. Resour., Utah Dept. of Nat. Resour., Salt Lake City, and Coop. Ext. Serv. and Dept. of Landscape Arch./Environ. Planning, Utah State Univ., Provo. 32 pp. Available from: Utah Division of Wildlife Resources, 1569 W. North Temple, Salt Lake City, UT 84116.

Phillips, H. R. 1985. Growing and propagating wild flowers. Univ. North Carolina Press, Chapel Hill. 331 pp.

Powers, V. S., and R. M. Hatcher. 1982. Giving wildlife an edge: a guide to ornamental plants for wildlife habitat. Tennessee Wildlife Resources Agency, P.O. Box 40747, Ellington Agricultural Center, Nashville, TN 37204. 44 pp.

Quinlan, S. E., and S. Cuccarese. 1982. Landscaping for wildlife in Alaska. Alaska Wildl. Watcher's Rep., Vol. 1, No. 2. Alaska Department of Fish and Game, 333 Raspberry Rd., Anchorage, AK 99502. 12 pp.

Sharp, W. C. 1977. Conservation plants for the Northeast. Program Aid 1154. Soil Conserv. Serv., U.S. Dept. Agric., Washington, D.C. 40 pp.

Smyser, C. A. 1982. Nature's design: a practical guide to natural landscaping. Rodale Press, Emmaus, Pennsylvania. 416 pp.

Soil and Water Conservation Society. 1987. Sources of native seeds and plants. Soil and Water Conservation Society, 7515 N.E. Ankeny Rd., Ankeny, IA 50021. 36 pp. (Lists addresses and phone numbers of suppliers by state, $3.00 postpaid.)

Soil Conservation Service. 1969. Invite birds to your home: conservation plantings for the Northeast. PA-940. Soil Conserv. Serv., U.S. Dept. Agric., Washington, D.C. 16-panel foldout.

Tekulsky, M. 1985. The butterfly garden. Harvard Common Press, Boston. 192 pp.

Tylka, D. n.d. Landscaping for backyard wildlife. Natural History Division, Missouri Conservation Dept., P.O. Box 180, Jefferson City, MO 65102. 11 pp.

Tylka, D. 1987. Butterfly gardening and conservation. Urban Wildl. Series—Pamphlet No. 2. Natural History Division, Missouri Conservation Dept., P.O. Box 180, Jefferson City, MO 65102. 17 pp.

Tylka, D., and J. Werner. 1983. Backyard bird feeding. Urban Wildl. Series—Pamphlet No. 1. Natural History Division, Missouri Conservation Dept. P.O. Box 180, Jefferson City, MO 65102. 8-panel foldout.

Underhill, J. E. 1980. Northwestern wild berries. Hancock House Publishers, North Vancouver, British Columbia. 96 pp.

Wasowski, S., and A. Wasowski. 1988. Native Texas plants, landscaping region by region. Texas Monthly Press, Inc., Austin. 304 pp.

Wilson, J. 1992. Landscaping with wildflowers: an environmental approach to gardening. Houghton Mifflin Co., Boston. 256 pp.

Wilson, W. H. W. 1984. Landscaping with wildflowers & native plants. Ortho Books, San Francisco, California. 93 pp.

Workman, R. W. 1980. Growing native: native plants for landscape use in coastal south Florida. Banyan Books, Miami, Florida. 137 pp.

Appendix B

Regional Listings of Selected Plants Ranked according to Their Value for Wildlife

Source: Martin et al. ([1951] 1961)

Northeast

Woody Plants

Oak *Quercus* spp.
Blackberry *Rubus* spp.
Wild Cherry *Prunus* spp.
Pine *Pinus* spp.
Dogwood *Cornus* spp.
Grape *Vitis* spp.
Maple *Acer* spp.
Beech *Fagus grandifolia*
Blueberry *Vaccinium* spp.
Birch *Betula* spp.
Sumac *Rhus* spp.
Aspen *Populus* spp.
Spruce *Picea* spp.
Hickory *Carya* spp.
Fir *Abies* spp.
Alder *Alnus* spp.
Poison Ivy *Toxicodendron radicans*
Blackgum *Nyssa sylvatica*
Mulberry *Morus* spp.
Elm *Ulmus* spp.
Cedar *Juniperus* spp.
Serviceberry *Amelanchier* spp.

Hazelnut *Corylus* spp.
Willow *Salix* spp.
Hemlock *Tsuga* spp.
Greenbrier *Smilax* spp.
Ash *Fraxinus* spp.
Elderberry *Sambucus* spp.
Virginia Creeper *Parthenocissus* spp.
Tulip Tree *Liriodendron tulipifera*
Mountain Ash *Sorbus* spp.
Holly *Ilex* spp.
Hawthorn *Crataegus* spp.
Black Walnut *Juglans nigra*

Herbaceous Plants

Ragweed *Ambrosia* spp.
Bristle Grass *Setaria* spp.
Sedge *Carex* spp.
Crabgrass *Digitaria* spp.
Panic grass *Panicum* spp.
Pigweed *Amaranthus* spp.
Clover *Trifolium* spp.
Sheep Sorrel *Rumex* spp.
Goosefoot *Chenopodium* spp.
Dropseed Grass *Sporobolus* spp.
Bluegrass *Poa* spp.

147

Pokeweed *Phytolacca americana*
Dandelion *Taraxacum* spp.
Plantain *Plantago* spp.

Southeast

Woody Plants

Oak
Pine
Blackberry
Wild Cherry
Greenbrier
Grape
Blueberry
Hickory
Blackgum
Holly
Poison Ivy
Beech
Maple
Virginia Creeper
Persimmon *Diospyros* spp.
Wax Myrtle *Myrica* spp.
Dogwood
Mulberry
Tulip Tree
Ash
Palmetto *Sabal* spp.
Sweetgum *Liquidambar styraciflua*
Elderberry
Cedar
Hackberry *Celtis* spp.
Swamp Ironwood *Cyrilla racemiflora*

Herbaceous Plants

Panic Grass
Bristle Grass
Ragweed

Paspalum *Paspalum* spp.
Crabgrass
Doveweed *Croton* spp.
Sedge
Pokeweed
Lespedeza *Lespedeza* spp.

Prairie

Woody Plants

Oak
Hackberry
Prickly Pear *Opuntia* spp.
Wild Rose *Rosa* spp.
Wild Cherry
Cedar
Grape
Sagebrush *Artemisia* spp.
Snowberry *Symphoricarpos* spp.
Sumac
Poison Ivy
Persimmon
Mulberry
Dogwood
Serviceberry
Saltbush *Atriplex* spp.
Holly
Blackberry
Pine
Mesquite *Prosopis* spp.
Alder
Barberry *Berberis* spp.
Bearberry *Arctostaphylos uva-ursi*
Virginia Creeper
Rabbitbrush *Chrysothamnus* spp.

Herbaceous Plants

Bristle Grass

Ragweed
Sunflower *Helianthus* spp.
Panic Grass
Knotweed *Polygonum* spp.
Pigweed
Doveweed
Goosefoot
Russian Thistle *Salsola kali*
Crabgrass
Dropseed Grass
Clover
Needlegrass *Stipa* spp.
Sedge
Fescue Grass *Festuca* spp.
Grama Grass *Bouteloua* spp.

Mountain-Desert

Woody Plants

Pine
Sagebrush
Mesquite
Prickly Pear
Oak
Cedar
Manzanita *Arctostaphylos* spp.
Douglas Fir *Pseudotsuga menziesii*
Wild Cherry
Serviceberry
Gooseberry *Ribes* spp.
Aspen
Hackberry
Saltbush
Fir
Willow
Birch
Blackberry
Rabbitbrush
Maple

Spruce
Bitterbrush *Purshia* spp.
Alder
Creosote *Larrea tridentata*
Elaeagnus *Elaeagnus* spp.
Blueberry
Buffaloberry *Shepherdia* spp.
Grape
Barberry

Herbaceous Plants

Bristle Grass
Pigweed
Sunflower
Ragweed
Sedge
Knotweed
Grama grass
Russian thistle
Dandelion
Filaree *Erodium* spp.
Goosefoot
Wheatgrass *Agropyron* spp.
Fescue Grass
Snakeweed *Gutierrezia* spp.
Bromegrass *Bromus* spp.
Deervetch *Lotus* spp.
Locoweed *Astragalus* spp.
Eriogonum *Eriogonum* spp.
Purslane *Portulaca* spp.
Bluegrass
Needlegrass
Doveweed
Tarweed *Madia* spp., *Hemizonia* spp.
Clover
Plantain
Spiderling *Boerhaavia* spp.
Fiddleneck *Amsinckia* spp.
Crownbeard *Verbesina encelioides*
Hilaria *Hilaria* spp.

Pacific

Woody Plants

Pine
Oak
Elderberry
Poison Oak *Toxicodendron
  diversilobum*
Blackberry
Manzanita
Buckthorn *Rhamnus* spp.
Wild Cherry
Prickly Pear
Ceanothus *Ceanothus* spp.
Cedar
Douglas Fir
Fir
Dogwood
Mesquite
Serviceberry
Spruce
Willow
Gooseberry
Snowberry
Bitterbrush
Alder
Birch
Sagebrush
Mistletoe *Loranthaceae*
Blueberry
Aspen
Mountain Mahogany
  Cercocarpus spp.

Salal *Gaultheria shallon*
Madrone *Arbutus* spp.
Buffaloberry

Herbaceous Plants

Wild Oats *Avena* spp.
Filaree
Pigweed
Bristle Grass
Turkey Mullein *Eremocarpus
  setigerus*
Knotweed
Tarweed
Red Maids *Calandrinia caulescens*
Bromegrass
Star Thistle *Centaurea* spp.
Sedge
Deervetch
Chickweed *Stellaria media*
Miner's Lettuce *Montia perfoliata*
Ragweed
Nightshade *Solanum* spp.
Fescue Grass
Clover
Sunflower
Lupine *Lupinus* spp.
Eriogonum
Goosefoot
Bur Clover *Medicago* spp.
Russian Thistle
Bluegrass
Fiddleneck

Appendix C

Glossary of Terms Used in the Text

Acid rain. Rainfall having increased acidity, resulting from mixture of upper atmosphere moisture with sulfur dioxide and nitrogen oxides (derived mainly from vehicle exhaust emissions and burning of coal) to produce sulfuric and nitric acids. Acid rain can kill trees and aquatic life, and there is concern that it may affect production of grains, vegetables, and other foods of humans.

Alarm call (and distress call). Vocalizations of an animal that warn other members of the population nearby of impending danger.

Alien. A plant or animal of foreign origin. The starling is an alien species in North America, having been introduced from Europe. (Compare with **indigenous species** and **invasive exotic species**.)

Aquifer. A rock formation capable of storing and transmitting groundwater.

Bask. To warm by exposure to an external heat source.

Bedrock. The solid rock underlying soils or other land surface materials.

Benthic organism. One that lives on the bottom of a stream, marsh, or lake.

Biological diversity. Sometimes shortened to "biodiversity." A recent term now widely used but having no unified definition. Generally encompasses genetic diversity, species diversity, and ecosystem diversity.

Browse. To feed on the tender young twigs and branches of shrubs and trees. In other usage, means the woody vegetation eaten as food by herbivores such as deer.

Carrying capacity. The population size of a species of interest that a given area of land can sustain over time. For many wildlife species in North America, restricted food during the winter season is a major determining factor.

Cavity tree. A living or dead tree with a hollow or partially hollow center in the main stem or major branches. Such cavities provide shelter and secluded places for many species, such as tree squirrels, to raise their young. See also **snag tree.**

Channelization. The straightening and deepening of a stream or river, removal of in-stream structures such as fallen trees, and removal of woody vegetation along the banks of a watercourse as a means of reducing floods. This practice is devastating to aquatic and riparian wildlife communities. Furthermore, the increased flow and volume of water through the channel may pose greater flooding risks to downstream areas. For these, and other, reasons the practice currently is not as widespread as it was in the recent past.

Chaparral. Low and often dense scrub vegetation characterized by shrubs or dwarf trees.

Cluster-type development. A method of distributing houses or other buildings on a given site in close association on reduced land area. Such development provides larger blocks of open space than does traditional development where buildings are evenly spaced throughout the entire site.

Coniferous forest. One consisting of evergreen trees such as pine, spruce, and fir.

Dabbling duck. A duck such as the mallard and wood duck that "tips up" to feed underwater in shallow areas. Most dabbling ducks utilize freshwater habitats and also are referred to as river ducks or puddle ducks.

Deciduous forest. One consisting of trees such as oak and hickory that lose their leaves in autumn.

Diked marsh. A marsh contained within the confines of a constructed earthen barrier (dike), usually with a device allowing the lowering or raising of water levels for management purposes.

Diversity. In general usage, species diversity, wildlife diversity, and plant diversity often refer to the number of species in an area. In the field of ecology, however, the term **species richness** is used to denote the total number of species of plants or animals, or both, in an area, and the term **diversity** more specifically refers to a mathematical "Species Diversity Index" that involves both the number of species and the relative numbers of each species.

Habitat diversity refers to the structure and composition of vegetation that forms potential habitats for wildlife. (See also **biological diversity.**)

Dust dome. Particulate matter in the atmosphere that tends to remain suspended in rising air currents above a city. (See **urban heat island.**)

Ecological range (and ecological tolerance). The varying environmental conditions under which an organism can survive and reproduce. For example, temperature extremes are important in defining ecological ranges of species.

Ecology. The science that studies organisms in relation to their environment and attempts to explain patterns and processes that make biological systems work.

Emergent vegetation. Aquatic plants, such as cattail and bulrush, that are rooted in bottom sediments of shallow waters with leaves and stems projecting vertically above the water surface. (Compare with **submerged aquatic vegetation.**)

Eutrophication. Nutrient enrichment. Term used in describing the process of natural or human-induced enrichment of a body of water with plant nutrients such as nitrogen and phosphorus. Eutrophic waters are fertile and productive.

Evapotranspiration. Water lost from the earth's surface by evaporation and plant transpiration.

Extirpation. The loss of a plant or animal species from a given area but not all areas. The mountain lion has been extirpated from much of the United States, although it still is present in many western states.

Fledging. Developmental stage in the life of a young bird when it becomes capable of flight.

Floodplain. Land area above the normal channel of a stream or river that becomes inundated with water following major rainstorms or rapid melting of snow.

Forb. A herbaceous plant that is not a grass nor grasslike. Many "weeds" are forbs.

Fossil fuel. Fuel extracted from the earth, such as coal.

Gene pool. All of the genes of interbreeding individuals of a population of a given species.

Gestation. Time period from egg fertilization until birth in mammals.

Greenhouse effect. Warming of the earth's atmosphere and land surface due to increased concentrations of atmospheric carbon dioxide and other gases that trap the infrared heat from the earth's surface as it is radiated back toward space. The process is similar to that which occurs in a glass greenhouse exposed to the sun.

Green space. Land surface covered by vegetation instead of asphalt, buildings, or other structures. Vegetation may consist of woody plants such as trees and shrubs or may be grass lawn. Green space may or may not be good wildlife habitat. (Compare with **open space.**)

Habitat generalist. A species that can find food, cover, and water under a variety of environmental conditions. Such a species has a broad ecological range and tolerance. The gray squirrel and raccoon are examples of habitat generalists. They can live in undeveloped forests as well as urban and suburban areas. (Compare with **habitat specialist.**)

Habitat management. The purposeful manipulation of the basic requirements of wildlife to meet human objectives. Most such effort deals with vegetation and water. Vegetation management involves manipulating plant species composition, structure, and pattern in the landscape. Various practices and techniques are used to provide and maintain water for wildlife. Manipulation of water levels in managed marshes is widely practiced to provide optimal food, cover, and nesting conditions for waterfowl.

Habitat specialist. A species that can find food, cover, and water only under a narrow range of environmental conditions. The black-footed ferret lives only in association with prairie dogs (its food source) in the western United States. With the loss of prairie habitat through conversion to crop production and grasslands, and subsequent reduction of its food supply, the ferret has become an endangered species. (Compare with **habitat generalist.**)

Habituate. To become accustomed to an unnatural stimulus. Canada geese and other birds feeding, nesting, or resting on airport grounds may become habituated to the noise of aircraft.

Hibernacula (singular: hibernaculum). The underground dens or other structures in which dormant animals pass the winter. Used mainly in reference to reptiles.

Home range. The area routinely traveled by an animal in its search for food, water, and shelter. Home range for a given species usually contracts when resources are abundant and expands when they become scarce. Typically, large animals and animals high in the food chain have larger ranges than do small animals and animals low in the food chain. Migratory species have summer ranges and winter ranges.

Humus layer. The top layer of soil consisting of partially decomposed plant or animal matter.

Hydrology. The science dealing with water—its properties, distribution, and circulation in the atmosphere, on land, and below the ground surface.

Indigenous species. Plants and animals that are native to a given country or continent. The bluebird is native to North America. (Compare with **alien** and **invasive exotic species.**)

Invasive exotic species. Plants or animals of foreign origin that take over niches formerly occupied by native species. Japanese honeysuckle is an invasive exotic plant in North America. (Compare with **alien** and **indigenous species.**)

Larvae. Immature forms of animals that differ markedly in size and shape from adults. Used mostly in reference to insects. Caterpillars are larvae of moths and butterflies.

Legume. A plant belonging to the pea family, such as white clover, alfalfa, and soybeans.

Litter. As used in the text, refers to the multiple young from a single birth of certain mammals (a litter of gray squirrels) or to the largely undecomposed dead leaves (leaf litter) and other plant material on the surface of the ground.

Marsh. A type of wetland characterized by shallow water and aquatic plants such as cattail and bulrush. There are freshwater marshes as well as saltwater marshes.

Mast. Nuts and fruits produced by trees and shrubs and utilized as food by wildlife. Acorns and hickory nuts are included in a group referred to as "hard mast," whereas "fleshy" fruits of dogwood and cherry are called "soft mast."

Mesophytic forest. A forest growing under medium conditions of moisture, not extremely wet or dry.

Mitigation. Avoidance of, or compensation for, damages to natural habitats, resulting from human developments.

Naturalistic landscaping. A landscape design created by humans with all or mostly native plant species and imitating natural habitat in appearance and function.

Neotropical migrant. A bird that breeds in North America and winters south of the Tropic of Cancer (roughly Central Mexico and Cuba southward and including South America).

Nursery stock. Young plants grown in confined spaces and generally under controlled or partially controlled environmental conditions for the purpose of transplanting to other sites for growth to maturity.

Open space. A term frequently substituted for "green space," but its meaning is broader in scope. Open space may include wooded stream valleys left intact after development as well as cemeteries, parking lots, and even indoor ice-skating rinks. Retention of open space in development plans does not necessarily mean retention of wildlife habitat. (Compare with **green space.**)

Organic matter. Material derived from plants and animals, including waste products as well as dead bodies of once-living organisms.

Ozone depletion. Loss of ozone (a form of oxygen that is a bluish gas) in the earth's upper atmosphere. A layer of ozone in the upper atmosphere blocks some of the sun's radiation from reaching the earth's surface. Chlorofluorocarbons, manufactured chemical compounds used as coolants in air conditioners and refrigerators and as propellants in aerosol spray cans, are largely responsible for such depletion. The chemicals float upward from the earth's surface and react with and destroy ozone. Ozone depletion leads to greater solar radiation at the ground surface, an increase that is detrimental to life processes. For example, increased radiation disrupts plant growth and causes skin cancer in humans.

Pocket park. A small park, usually found in densely developed portions of cities where competition for space is intense.

Porous pavement. A type of road, driveway, or parking-lot surface that allows water from rainfall or snowfall to infiltrate the ground below. Typical asphalt or concrete pavement provides a barrier to such water absorption.

Prairie Pothole Region. Grassland region of the northcentral United States and southern Canada where small, shallow ponds and marshes were formed by Pleistocene glaciation. Sometimes called a "duck factory" because of its value to breeding ducks.

Raptor. A bird of prey, such as a hawk, an eagle, or an owl.

River delta. The flat, or nearly flat, landform created by the deposition of sediment at the mouth of a river.

Rooftop garden. Green space developed on the flat rooftop of a building. Such sites represent the greatest area of vacant space in the inner core of most cities. Vegetation can be selected for its value to wildlife.

Shelterbelt. A strip of trees and/or shrubs planted between fields to protect farmland from wind erosion. Such an area also provides habitat to wildlife.

Short-rotation pine plantation. An area where pines are grown for commercial purposes and harvested in a relatively short time span. The area is then replanted with tree seedlings. In the southeastern United States, trees grown for pulpwood are typically on a rotation of about 25 to 30 years.

Snag tree. A standing dead or dying tree. Such trees are valuable to wildlife, particularly birds, in providing food (insects) and nesting sites for woodpeckers, chickadees, wood ducks, and screech owls, among others.

Soil amendment. A substance such as fertilizer or lime added to soil to enhance growing conditions for plants.

Soil microbes. Very small organisms, including bacteria, that live in the soil.

Solar radiation. Radiation from the sun.

Species richness. The total number of species of plants or animals, or both, in an area. (See **diversity.**)

Submerged aquatic vegetation. Aquatic plants that lie entirely beneath the water surface. (Compare with **emergent vegetation.**)

Thermoregulation. Capability of certain species, mostly birds and mammals, to maintain relatively stable body temperatures from heat produced by their own internal metabolism and sufficient insulation (such as feathers and fur) to help control heat loss.

Tidal flat. The level or nearly level land surface, typically consisting of mud or sand, that lies between high and low tides of marine and estuarine waters.

Tree pit. A hole designed for a tree along a city street and sidewalk. Generally, the ground surface surrounding the pit is completely covered by concrete and/or asphalt. Trees have a difficult time growing under such harsh conditions where moisture and root space are limited.

Tree wrap. Commercially available material used to wrap the trunks of newly planted trees to repel gnawing rodents and rabbits.

Tundra. Treeless land in arctic and alpine regions that may contain grasses, sedges, forbs, dwarf shrubs, mosses, and lichens.

Understory. Vegetation below the tree canopy in a forest. This structural element of the forest is valuable to many wildlife species.

Urban heat island. Term used to characterize the atmospheric temperature differential between a city and the surrounding countryside. Air temperature is warmer in the city largely as a result of the storage of solar radiation in brick, concrete, and asphalt and slow loss of this heat back to the atmosphere. In many areas, loss of trees in the city contributes to the urban heat island effect.

Urban wildlife. Nondomestic vertebrates and invertebrates of urban, suburban, and urbanizing areas.

Vascular plant. One with internal "vessels" for transporting water as well as nutrients and other substances in a fluid form. Included are ferns and seed plants from delicate lilies to towering oaks.

Vegetation composition. The different kinds of plant species within a given area and their relative abundance.

Vegetation structure. The physical distribution and form of plant species within a given area. Horizontal structure refers to the pattern of vegetation distribution across the landscape, whereas vertical structure refers to different layers of vegetation from the ground to the tree canopy.

Watershed. The area drained by a given river or stream system.

Weathering. Environmental processes that lead to decomposition of bedrock and formation of soil.

References

Abbott, C. G. 1930. Urban burrowing owls. Auk 47:564–565.

Adamec, R. E. 1976. The interaction of hunger and preying in the domestic cat: an adaptive hierarchy? Behav. Biol. 18:263–272.

Adams, L. W., and L. E. Dove. 1989. Wildlife reserves and corridors in the urban environment. Natl. Inst. for Urban Wildl., Columbia, Maryland. 91 pp.

Adams, L. W., L. E. Dove, and T. M. Franklin. 1985a. Mallard pair and brood use of urban stormwater-control impoundments. Wildl. Soc. Bull. 13:46–51.

Adams, L. W., L. E. Dove, and T. M. Franklin. 1985b. Use of urban stormwater control impoundments by wetland birds. Wilson Bull. 97:120–122.

Adams, L. W., T. M. Franklin, L. E. Dove, and J. M. Duffield. 1986. Design considerations for wildlife in urban stormwater management. Trans. North Am. Wildl. and Nat. Resour. Conf. 51:249–259.

Adams, L. W., C. D. Rhodehamel, and J. S. McKegg. 1987. A strategy for managing urban waterfowl populations. Page 235 in L. W. Adams and D. L. Leedy, eds. Integrating man and nature in the metropolitan environment. Natl. Inst. for Urban Wildl., Columbia, Maryland.

Aguilera, E., R. L. Knight, and J. L. Cummings. 1991. An evaluation of two hazing methods for urban Canada geese. Wildl. Soc. Bull. 19:32–35.

Aldrich, J. W., and R. W. Coffin. 1980. Breeding bird populations from forest to suburbia after thirty-seven years. Am. Birds 34:3–7.

Allen, D. L. 1962. Our wildlife legacy. Funk & Wagnalls, New York. 422 pp.

Andelt, W. F., and B. R. Mahan. 1980. Behavior of an urban coyote. Am. Midland Nat. 103:399–400.

Anderson, J. W. 1979. The burrowing owl in Sacramento. Bull. Sacramento Zool. Soc. 16:9–12.

Anderson, L. M., B. E. Mulligan, and L. S. Goodman. 1984. Effects of vegetation on human response to sound. J. Arboriculture 10:45–49.

Andriot, J. L. 1983. Population abstract of the United States. Vol. 1. Tables. Andriot Assoc., McLean, Virginia. 895 pp.

Anonymous. 1989. Tinicum National Environmental Center brochure. U.S. Fish and Wildl. Serv., Tinicum Natl. Environ. Cent., Philadelphia, Pennsylvania.

159

160   References

Arnold, R. A., and A. E. Goins. 1987. Habitat enhancement techniques for the El Segundo blue butterfly: an urban endangered species. Pages 173-181 *in* L. W. Adams and D. L. Leedy, eds. Integrating man and nature in the metropolitan environment. Natl. Inst. for Urban Wildl., Columbia, Maryland.

Aurelia, M. A. 1987. The role of wetland regulation in preserving wildlife habitat in suburban environments. Pages 213-219 *in* L. W. Adams and D. L. Leedy, eds. Integrating man and nature in the metropolitan environment. Natl. Inst. for Urban Wildl., Columbia, Maryland.

Barber, J. C., and M. M. Barber. 1988. Prey of an urban peregrine falcon—Part II. Maryland Birdlife 44:37-39.

Barbour, D. A. 1986. Why are there so few butterflies in Liverpool? An answer. Antenna 10:72-75.

Bascietto, J. J., and L. W. Adams. 1983. Frogs and toads of stormwater management basins in Columbia, Maryland. Bull. Md. Herpetol. Soc. 19:58-60.

Bassuk, N., and T. Whitlow. 1987. Environmental stress in street trees. Pages 49-57 *in* P. R. Thoday and D. W. Robinson, eds. The scientific management of vegetation in the urban environment. Acta Horticulturae 195. Inst. Soc. for Horticultural Sci., Wageningen, The Netherlands.

Beck, A. M. 1974. The ecology of urban dogs. Pages 57-59 *in* J. H. Noyes and D. R. Progulske, eds. Wildlife in an urbanizing environment. Plan. and Resour. Dev. Ser. No. 28. Holdsworth Natural Resources Center, Univ. Massachusetts, Amherst.

Beissinger, S. R., and D. R. Osborne. 1982. Effects of urbanization on avian community organization. Condor 84:75-83.

Bellrose, F. C. 1976. Ducks, geese and swans of North America. Stackpole Books, Harrisburg, Pennsylvania. 544 pp.

Berger, D. D., C. R. Sindelar, Jr., and K. E. Gamble. 1969. The status of breeding peregrines in the eastern United States. Pages 165-173 *in* J. J. Hickey, ed. Peregrine falcon populations: their biology and decline. Univ. of Wisconsin Press, Madison.

Bezzel, E. 1985. Birdlife in intensively used rural and urban environments. Ornis Fennica 62:90-95.

Bissell, S. J., K. Demarest, and D. L. Schrupp. 1987. The use of zoning ordinances in the protection and development of wildlife habitat. Pages 37-42 *in* L. W. Adams and D. L. Leedy, eds. Integrating man and nature in the metropolitan environment. Natl. Inst. for Urban Wildl., Columbia, Maryland.

Block, B. C. 1966. Williamsport, Pennsylvania, tries starling control with distress calls. Pest Control 34:24-30.

Bloomfield, H. E., J. F. Handley, and A. D. Bradshaw. 1982. Nutrient deficiencies and the aftercare of reclaimed derelict land. J. Applied Ecol. 19:151-158.

Boddicker, M. L. 1983. Prairie dogs. Pages B-75 through B-84 *in* R. M. Timm, ed. Prevention and control of wildlife damage. Great Plains Agric. Council Wildl. Resour. Comm. and Nebraska Coop. Ext. Serv., Univ. of Nebraska, Lincoln.

Bollengier, R. M., Jr. 1983. Woodchucks. Pages B-153 through B-156 *in* R. M. Timm, ed. Prevention and control of wildlife damage. Great Plains Agric. Council Wildl. Resour. Comm. and Nebraska Coop. Ext. Serv., Univ. Nebraska, Lincoln.

Boone, D. D. 1979. Homes for birds. Conserv. Bull. 14. rev. ed. U.S. Fish and Wildl. Serv., Washington, D.C. 22 pp.

Booth, M., and M. M. Allen. 1990. Butterfly garden design. Pages 69-93 *in* L. Gunnarson and F. Haselsteiner, eds. Butterfly gardening: creating summer magic in your garden. Sierra Club Books, San Francisco, California.

Booth, T. W. 1983. Bird dispersal techniques. Pages E-1 through E-5 *in* R. M. Timm, ed. Prevention and control of wildlife damage. Great Plains Agric. Council Wildl. Resour. Comm. and Nebraska Coop. Ext. Serv., Univ. Nebraska, Lincoln.

Boyer, M. G., M. Hough, and C. Furedy. 1986. Rehabilitation of forested areas in an urban setting. Environ. Conserv. 13:263-265.

Bradshaw, A. D. 1982. The biology of land reclamation in urban areas. Pages 293-303 *in* R. Bornkamm, J. A. Lee, and M. R. D. Seaward, eds. Urban ecology. Blackwell Sci. Publ., Oxford, United Kingdom.

Brand, C. J. 1987. Duck plague. Pages 117-127 *in* M. Friend, ed. Field guide to wildlife diseases. Vol. I. General field procedures and diseases of migratory birds. Resour. Publ. 167. U.S. Fish and Wildl. Serv., Washington, D.C.

Breitwisch, R., and M. Breitwisch. 1991. House sparrows open an automatic door. Wilson Bull. 103:725-726.

Brittingham, M. C. 1991. Effects of winter bird feeding on wild birds. Pages 185-190 *in* L. W. Adams and D. L. Leedy, eds. Wildlife conservation in metropolitan environments. Natl. Inst. for Urban Wildlife, Columbia, Maryland.

Brittingham, M. C., and S. A. Temple. 1983. Have cowbirds caused forest songbirds to decline? BioScience 33:31-35.

Brittingham, M. C., and S. A. Temple. 1988a. Impacts of supplemental feeding on survival rates of black-capped chickadees. Ecology 69:581-589.

Brittingham, M. C., and S. A. Temple. 1988b. Avian disease and winter bird feeding. The Passenger Pigeon 50:195-203.

Brown, L. R., and J. L. Jacobson. 1987. The future of urbanization: facing the ecological and economic constraints. Worldwatch Paper 77. Worldwatch Institute, Washington, D.C. 58 pp.

Brush, C. C., and D. W. Ehrenfeld. 1991. Control of white-tailed deer in non-hunted reserves and urban fringe areas. Pages 59-66 *in* L. W. Adams and D. L. Leedy, eds. Wildlife conservation in metropolitan environments. Natl. Inst. for Urban Wildl., Columbia, Maryland.

Bryant, B. K., and W. Ishmael. 1991. Movement and mortality patterns of resident and translocated suburban white-tailed deer. Pages 53-58 *in* L. W. Adams and D. L. Leedy, eds. Wildlife conservation in metropolitan environments. Natl. Inst. for Urban Wildl., Columbia, Maryland.

Bryson, R. A., and J. E. Ross. 1972. The climate of the city. Pages 51-68 *in* T. R. Detwyler and M. G. Marcus, eds. Urbanization and environment. Duxbury Press, Belmont, California.

Burns, J., K. Stenberg, and W. W. Shaw. 1986. Critical and sensitive wildlife habitats in Tucson, Arizona. Pages 144-150 *in* K. Stenberg and W. W. Shaw, eds. Wildlife conservation and new residential developments. School of Renewable Nat. Resour., Univ. Arizona, Tucson.

Burr, R. M., and R. E. Jones. 1968. The influence of parkland habitat management on birds in Delaware. Trans. North Am. Wildl. and Nat. Resour. Conf. 33:299-306.

Bustad, L. K. 1987. Historical perspective. Pages 19-20 *in* Health benefits of pets: program and abstracts. NIH Technology Assessment Workshop, 10-11 September, Bethesda, Maryland.

Byers, S. M., R. A. Montgomery, and G. V. Burger. 1987. An assessment of wildlife and wildlife habitat in Kane County, Illinois. Page 238 *in* L. W. Adams and D. L. Leedy, eds. Integrating man and nature in the metropolitan environment. Natl. Inst. for Urban Wildl., Columbia, Maryland.

Cade, T. J., and D. M. Bird. 1990. Peregrine falcons, *Falco peregrinus,* nesting in an urban environment: a review. Can. Field-Nat. 104:209-218.

Cadieux, C. L. 1987. Pronghorn antelope: great plains rebound. Pages 133-143 *in* H. Kallman, ed. Restoring America's wildlife 1937-1987. U.S. Fish and Wildl. Serv., Washington, D.C.

Calhoon, R. E., and C. Haspel. 1989. Urban cat populations compared by season, subhabitat and supplemental feeding. J. Animal Ecol. 58:321-328.

Campbell, C. A. 1974. Survival of reptiles and amphibians in urban environments. Pages 61-66 in J. H. Noyes and D. R. Progulske, eds. Wildlife in an urbanizing environment. Plan. and Resour. Dev. Ser. No. 28. Holdsworth Natural Resources Center, Univ. Massachusetts, Amherst.

Carl, L. M., J. R. Ryckman, and W. C. Latta. 1976. Management of trout fishing in a metropolitan area. Michigan Dept. Nat. Resour., Fish. Div., Fish. Res. Rep. 1836. 29 pp.

Case, R. M. 1983. Pocket gophers. Pages B-13 through B-26 in R. M. Timm, ed. Prevention and control of wildlife damage. Great Plains Agric. Council Wildl. Resour. Comm. and Nebraska Coop. Ext. Serv., Univ. Nebraska, Lincoln.

Chevalier, S. 1988. Snowy owl populations at Kennedy International Airport, New York: a twenty-three year study. North Am. Bird Bander 13:2-3.

Christie, R. G., M. W. Sayre, and D. R. Progulske. 1987. Deer movements and habitat use on the Morristown National Historic Park: implications for management of a suburban island population. Trans. NE Sect. The Wildl. Soc. 44:88. Abstract only.

Churcher, P. B., and J. H. Lawton. 1989. Beware of well-fed felines. Natural History, July, pp. 40-47.

City of Toledo, Iowa. 1987. Application for certification of Toledo Heights Park as an urban wildlife sanctuary. Natl. Inst. for Urban Wildl., Columbia, Maryland.

Cochran, P. A. 1989. Historical changes in a suburban herpetofauna in DuPage County, Illinois. Bull. Chicago Herpetol. Soc. 24:1-7.

Colvin, B. A. 1985. Common barn-owl population decline in Ohio and the relationship to agricultural trends. J. Field Ornithol. 56:224-235.

Conover, M. R. 1984. Effectiveness of repellents in reducing deer damage in nurseries. Wildl. Soc. Bull. 12:399-404.

Conover, M. R., and G. S. Kania. 1988. Browsing preference of white-tailed deer for different ornamental species. Wildl. Soc. Bull. 16:175-179.

Cook, R. P., and C. A. Pinnock. 1987. Recreating a herpetofaunal community at Gateway National Recreation Area. Pages 151-154 in L. W. Adams and D. L. Leedy, eds. Integrating man and nature in the metropolitan environment. Natl. Inst. for Urban Wildl., Columbia, Maryland.

Cooper, J. A. 1987. The effectiveness of translocation control of Minneapolis–St. Paul Canada goose populations. Pages 169-171 in L. W. Adams and D. L. Leedy, eds. Integrating man and nature in the metropolitan environment. Natl. Inst. for Urban Wildl., Columbia, Maryland.

Cooper, J. A. 1991. Canada goose management at the Minneapolis–St. Paul international airport. Pages 175-183 in L. W. Adams and D. L. Leedy, eds. Wildlife conservation in metropolitan environments. Natl. Inst. for Urban Wildl., Columbia, Maryland.

Courtsal, F. R. 1983. Pigeons (rock doves). Pages E-35 through E-41 in R. M. Timm, ed. Prevention and control of wildlife damage. Great Plains Agric. Council Wildl. Resour. Comm. and Nebraska Coop. Ext. Serv., Univ. Nebraska, Lincoln.

Craul, P. J. 1985. A description of urban soils and their desired characteristics. J. Arboriculture 11:330-339.

Craven, S. R. 1983a. Cottontail rabbits. Pages D-69 through D-74 in R. M. Timm, ed. Prevention and control of wildlife damage. Great Plains Agric. Council Wildl. Resour. Comm. and Nebraska Coop. Ext. Serv., Univ. Nebraska, Lincoln.

Craven, S. R. 1983b. Deer. Pages D-23 through D-33 in R. M. Timm, ed. Prevention and control of wildlife damage. Great Plains Agric. Council Wildl. Resour. Comm. and Nebraska Coop. Ext. Serv., Univ. Nebraska, Lincoln.

Craven, S. R. 1983c. Thirteen-lined ground squirrels. Pages B-137 through B-140 *in* R. M. Timm, ed. Prevention and control of wildlife damage. Great Plains Agric. Council Wildl. Resour. Comm. and Nebraska Coop. Ext. Serv., Univ. Nebraska, Lincoln.

Dasmann, R. F. 1966. Wildlife and the new conservation. Wildl. Soc. News 105:48–49.

Davis, D. D., and H. D. Gerhold. 1976. Selection of trees for tolerance of air pollutants. Pages 61–66 *in* F. S. Santamour, Jr., H. D. Gerhold, and S. Little, eds. Better trees for metropolitan landscapes. USDA For. Serv. Gen. Tech. Rep. NE-22, U.S. Gov. Print. Off., Washington, D.C.

Dawson, K. J. 1988. Flight, fancy, and the garden's song. Landscape Journal 7:170–175.

Dawson, K. J. 1991. Human predation on isolated nature reserves. Pages 83–88 *in* L. W. Adams and D. L. Leedy, eds. Wildlife conservation in metropolitan environments. Natl. Inst. for Urban Wildl., Columbia, Maryland.

de Almeida, M. H. 1987. Nuisance furbearer damage control in urban and suburban areas. Pages 996–1006 *in* M. Novak, J. A. Baker, M. E. Obbard, and B. Malloch, eds. Wild furbearer management and conservation in North America. Ontario Trappers Assoc., North Bay, Canada.

DeGraaf, R. M. 1987. Urban wildlife habitat research—application to landscape design. Pages 107–111 *in* L. W. Adams and D. L. Leedy, eds. Integrating man and nature in the metropolitan environment. Natl. Inst. for Urban Wildl., Columbia, Maryland.

DeGraaf, R. M., and J. M. Wentworth. 1981. Urban bird communities and habitats in New England. Trans. North Am. Wildl. and Nat. Resour. Conf. 46:396–413.

Demgen, F. C. 1988. A review of eighteen wetland mitigation sites in the San Francisco Bay region. Pages 318–322 *in* J. A. Kusler, S. Daly, and G. Brooks, eds. Urban wetlands: proceedings of the national wetland symposium. Assoc. of Wetland Managers, Berne, New York.

DesJardine, R. L. 1984. Fish stocking, an aspect of urban fisheries management. Pages 118–131 *in* L. J. Allen, ed. Urban fishing symposium proceedings. Fish. Manage. Sect. and Fish. Admin. Sect., Am. Fish. Soc., Bethesda, Maryland.

Dewers, R. S. 1981. Evaluation of native and exotic woody plants under severe environmental stress. J. Arboriculture 7:299–302.

Diemer, J. E. 1987. The status of the gopher tortoise in Florida. Pages 72–83 *in* R. R. Odom, K. A. Riddleberger, and J. C. Ozier, eds. Proceedings of the third southeastern nongame and endangered wildlife symposium. Georgia Dept. Nat. Resour., Social Circle.

Dirr, M. A. 1976. Salts and woody-plant interactions in the urban environment. Pages 103–111 *in* F. S. Santamour, Jr., H. D. Gerhold, and S. Little, eds. Better trees for metropolitan landscapes. USDA For. Serv. Gen. Tech. Rep. NE-22. U.S. Gov. Print. Off., Washington, D.C.

Dirr, M. A. 1978. Tolerance of seven woody ornamentals to soil-applied sodium chloride. J. Arboriculture 4:162–165.

Dixon, J. 1927. A lesson in civic ornithology. Bird-Lore 29:329–334.

Dorney, J. R., G. R. Guntenspergen, J. R. Keough, and F. Stearns. 1984. Composition and structure of an urban woody plant community. Urban Ecol. 8:69–90.

Duttweiler, M. W. 1975. Urban sport fishing: a review of literature and programs. New York Coop. Fish Res. Unit, Cornell Univ. Press, Ithaca. 52 pp.

Emlen, J. T. 1974. An urban bird community in Tucson, Arizona: derivation, structure, regulation. Condor 76:184–197.

Faeth, S. H., and T. C. Kane. 1978. Urban biogeography: city parks as islands for Diptera and Coleoptera. Oecologia 32:127–133.

Fagen, R. M. 1978. Domestic cat demography and population genetics in a midwestern U.S.A. metropolitan area. Carnivore 1:60–67.

Falk, J. H. 1976. Energetics of a suburban lawn ecosystem. Ecology 57:141–150.

Falk, J. H. 1977. The frenetic life forms that flourish in suburban lawns. Smithsonian 8:90–96.

Falk, J. H. 1980. The primary productivity of lawns in a temperate environment. J. Applied Ecol. 17:689–696.

Farnsworth, N. R. 1988. Screening plants for new medicines. Pages 83–97 *in* E. O. Wilson, ed. Biodiversity. Natl. Acad. Press, Washington, D.C.

Figley, W. K., and L. W. VanDruff. 1982. The ecology of urban mallards. Wildl. Monogr. 81. 40 pp.

Filion, F. L., et al. 1983. The importance of wildlife to Canadians: highlights of the 1981 national survey. Cat. No. CW66–62/1983E. Canadian Wildl. Serv., Ottawa, Ontario. 40 pp.

Fisk, E. J. 1978. The growing use of roofs by nesting birds. Bird-Banding 49:135–141.

Fitzwater, W. D. 1983. House sparrows. Pages E–43 through E–51 *in* R. M. Timm, ed. Prevention and control of wildlife damage. Great Plains Agric. Council Wildl. Resour. Comm. and Nebraska Coop. Ext. Serv., Univ. Nebraska, Lincoln.

Fletcher, J. L., and R. G. Busnel, eds. 1978. Effects of noise on wildlife. Academic Press, Inc., New York. 305 pp.

Flyger, V. 1959. A comparison of methods for estimating squirrel populations. J. Wildl. Manage. 23:220–223.

Flyger, V. 1974. Tree squirrels in urbanizing environments. Pages 121–124 *in* J. H. Noyes and D. R. Progulske, eds. Wildlife in an urbanizing environment. Plan. and Resour. Dev. Ser. No. 28. Holdsworth Natural Resources Center, Univ. Massachusetts, Amherst.

Frankie, G. W., and L. E. Ehler. 1978. Ecology of insects in urban environments. Annu. Rev. Entomol. 23:367–387.

Franklin, T. M., and L. W. Adams. 1980. Bird response to habitat improvement in an urban environment. Maryland Birdlife 36:14–16.

Fredrickson, L. H., and T. S. Taylor. 1982. Management of seasonally flooded impoundments for wildlife. Resour. Publ. 148. U.S. Fish and Wildl. Serv., Washington, D.C. 29 pp.

Frings, H., and J. Jumber. 1954. Preliminary studies on the use of a specific sound to repel starlings *(Sturnus vulgaris)* from objectionable roosts. Science 119:318–319.

Gause, G. F. [1934] 1964. The struggle for existence. Hafner Publishing Co., New York. 163 pp.

Gavareski, C. A. 1976. Relation of park size and vegetation to urban bird populations in Seattle, Washington. Condor 78:375–382.

Gavett, A. P., and J. S. Wakeley. 1986. Diets of house sparrows in urban and rural habitats. Wilson Bull. 98:137–144.

Geggie, J. F., and M. B. Fenton. 1985. A comparison of foraging by *Eptesicus fuscus* (Chiroptera: Vespertilionidae) in urban and rural environments. Can. J. Zool. 63:263–266.

Gehlbach, F. R. 1986. Odd couples of suburbia. Nat. History 95:56–66.

Gehlbach, F. R. 1988. Population and environmental features that promote adaptation to urban ecosystems: the case of eastern screech-owls *(Otus asio)* in Texas. Proc. Intl. Ornithol. Congress 19:1809–1813.

Geis, A. D. 1974. Effects of urbanization and type of urban development on bird populations. Pages 97–105 *in* J. H. Noyes and D. R. Progulske, eds. A symposium on wildlife in an urbanizing environment. Plan. and Resour. Dev. Ser. 28. Holdsworth Natural Resources Center, Univ. Massachusetts, Amherst.

Geis, A. D. 1976. Effects of building design and quality on nuisance bird problems. Proc. Vert. Pest Conf. 7:51–53.

Geis, A. D. 1980. Relative attractiveness of different foods at wild bird feeders. Special Sci. Rep. — Wildl. #233. U.S. Fish and Wildl. Serv., Washington, D.C.

Gennaro, A. L. 1988a. Breeding biology of an urban population of Mississippi kites in New Mexico. Pages 188-190 *in* R. L. Glinski, et al., eds. Proc. of the southwest raptor management symposium and workshop. Sci. Tech. Ser. 11. Natl. Wildl. Fed., Washington, D.C.

Gennaro, A. L. 1988b. Extent and control of aggressive behavior toward humans by Mississippi kites. Pages 249-252 *in* R. L. Glinski, et al., eds. Proc. of the southwest raptor management symposium and workshop. Sci. Tech. Ser. 11. Natl. Wildl. Fed., Washington, D.C.

Gill, D., and P. Bonnett. 1973. Nature in the urban landscape: a study of city ecosystems. York Press, Inc., Baltimore, Maryland. 209 pp.

Glahn, J. F., A. R. Stickley, Jr., J. F. Heisterberg, and D. F. Mott. 1991. Impact of roost control on local urban and agricultural blackbird problems. Wildl. Soc. Bull. 19:511-522.

Glinski, R. L., and A. L. Gennaro. 1988. Mississippi kite. Pages 54-56 *in* R. L. Glinski, et al., eds. Proc. of the southwest raptor management symposium and workshop. Sci. Tech. Ser. 11. Natl. Wildl. Fed., Washington, D.C.

Gold, S. M. 1986. User characteristics and response to vegetation in neighbourhood parks. Arboricultural Journal 10:275-287.

Goldstein, E. L., M. Gross, and R. M. DeGraaf. 1981. Explorations in bird-land geometry. Urban Ecol. 5:113-124.

Goldstein, E. L., M. Gross, and R. M. DeGraaf. 1983. Wildlife and greenspace planning in medium-scale residential developments. Urban Ecol. 7:201-214.

Goode, D. A. 1991. Wildlife in cities. Pages 7-21 *in* E. A. Webb and S. Q. Foster, eds. Perspectives in urban ecology. Denver Mus. of Nat. Hist., Denver, Colorado.

Gowaty, P. A. 1984. House sparrows kill eastern bluebirds. J. Field Ornith. 55:378-380.

Greenhall, A. M. 1982. House bat management. Resour. Publ. 143. U.S. Fish and Wildl. Serv., Washington, D.C. 33 pp.

Grobecker, D. B., and T. W. Pietsch. 1978. Crows use automobiles as nutcrackers. Auk 95:760.

Happe, P. J. 1982. The use of suburban habitats by Columbian black-tailed deer. M.S. thesis, Oregon State Univ., Corvallis. 95 pp.

Harris, L. D. 1984. The fragmented forest: island biogeography theory and the preservation of biotic diversity. Univ. Chicago Press, Chicago, Illinois. 211 pp.

Harris, S., and J. M. V. Rayner. 1986. Urban fox *(Vulpes vulpes)* population estimates and habitat requirements in several British cities. J. Anim. Ecol. 55:575-591.

Hartman, D. S. 1979. Ecology and behavior of the manatee *(Trichechus manatus)* in Florida. Am. Soc. Mammalogists Spec. Publ. 5. 153 pp.

Hathaway, M. B. 1973. Ecology of city squirrels. Nat. Hist. 82:61-62.

Hawkins, A. S. 1970. Honkers move to the city. Pages 120-130 *in* H. H. Dill and F. B. Lee, eds. Home grown honkers. U.S. Dept. Inter., Fish and Wildl. Serv., Washington, D.C.

Hawkins, A. S., L. R. Bradley, and R. H. Cunningham. 1990. Producing urban and suburban wood ducks. Pages 255-257 *in* L. H. Fredrickson, et al., eds. 1988 North American wood duck symposium, St. Louis, Missouri.

Hench, J. E., K. V. Ness, and R. Gibbs. 1987. Development of a natural resources planning and management process. Pages 29-35 *in* L. W. Adams and D. L. Leedy, eds. Integrating man and nature in the metropolitan environment. Natl. Inst. for Urban Wildl., Columbia, Maryland.

Henderson, C. L. 1984. Woodworking for wildlife: homes for birds and mammals. Minnesota Dept. Nat. Resour., St. Paul.

Henderson, F. R. 1983. Moles. Pages D-53 through D-61 *in* R. M. Timm, ed. Prevention and control of wildlife damage. Great Plains Agric. Council Wildl. Resour. Comm. and Nebraska Coop. Ext. Serv., Univ. Nebraska, Lincoln.

Herold, L. C. 1991. The urban climate. Pages 35–44 *in* E. A. Webb and S. Q. Foster, eds. Perspectives in urban ecology. Denver Mus. of Nat. Hist., Denver, Colorado.

Heusmann, H W. 1981. Movements and survival rates of park mallards. J. Field Ornithol. 52:214–221.

Heusmann, H W, and R. Burrell. 1984. Park waterfowl populations in Massachusetts. J. Field Ornithol. 55:89–96.

Hickey, J. J. 1942. Eastern population of the duck hawk. Auk 59:176–204.

Hodge, G. R., ed. 1990. Pocket guide to the humane control of wildlife in cities & towns. The Humane Society of the United States, Washington, D.C. 112 pp.

Hodgson, J. G. 1986. Commonness and rarity in plants with special reference to the Sheffield flora. Part I: the identity, distribution and habitat characteristics of the common and rare species. Biol. Conserv. 36:199–252.

Hoehne, L. M. 1981. The groundlayer vegetation of forest islands in an urban-suburban matrix. Pages 41–54 *in* R. L. Burgess and D. M. Sharpe, eds. Forest island dynamics in man-dominated landscapes. Springer-Verlag, New York.

Hoffmann, C. O., and J. L. Gottschang. 1977. Numbers, distribution, and movements of a raccoon population in a suburban residential community. J. Mammal. 58:623–636.

Holm, P. A. 1988. Two populations of the tree lizard *(Urosaurus ornatus)* in southern Arizona. M.S. thesis, Univ. Arizona, Tucson. 107 pp.

Hopkins, D. D., and R. B. Forbes. 1979. Size and reproductive patterns of the Virginia opossum in northwestern Oregon. Murrelet 60:95–98.

Hopkins, D. D., and R. B. Forbes. 1980. Dietary patterns of the Virginia opossum in an urban environment. Murrelet 61:20–30.

Houck, M. C. 1991. Metropolitan wildlife refuge system: a strategy for regional natural resource planning. Pages 225–229 *in* L. W. Adams and D. L. Leedy, eds. Wildlife conservation in metropolitan environments. Natl. Inst. for Urban Wildl., Columbia, Maryland.

Huang, Y. J., H. Akbari, H. Taha, and A. H. Rosenfeld. 1987. The potential of vegetation in reducing summer cooling loads in residential buildings. J. Climate and Applied Meteorology 26:1103–1116.

Hudson, J. L. 1984. Urban trout fishery. Page 292 *in* L. J. Allen, ed. Urban fishing symposium proceedings. Fish. Manage. Sect. and Fish. Admin. Sect., Am. Fish. Soc., Bethesda, Maryland. Abstract only.

Jackson, J. A. 1992. Crafty mudslinger: an appreciation of the cosmopolitan barn swallow. Birder's World 6:12–16.

James, P. C. 1988. Urban merlins in Canada. Brit. Birds 81:274–277.

Johnsen, A. M., and L. W. VanDruff. 1987. Summer and winter distribution of introduced bird species and native bird species richness within a complex urban environment. Pages 123–127 *in* L. W. Adams and D. L. Leedy, eds. Integrating man and nature in the metropolitan environment. Natl. Inst. for Urban Wildl., Columbia, Maryland.

Johnson, L., and G. Jackson. 1980. Construction site erosion control: how local government can solve the problem. Bull. No. A3076. Univ. Wisconsin Coop. Ext. Serv., Madison.

Johnson, R. J., and J. F. Glahn. 1983. Starlings. Pages E-53 through E-65 *in* R. M. Timm, ed. Prevention and control of wildlife damage. Great Plains Agric. Council Wildl. Resour. Comm. and Nebraska Coop. Ext. Serv., Univ. Nebraska, Lincoln.

Johnson, R. J., P. H. Cole, and W. W. Stroup. 1985. Starling response to three auditory stimuli. J. Wildl. Manage. 49:620–625.

Jones, J. M., and J. H. Witham. 1990. Post-translocation survival and movements of metropolitan white-tailed deer. Wildl. Soc. Bull. 18:434–441.

Jones, R. C., and C. C. Clark. 1987. Impact of watershed urbanization on stream insect communities. Water Resour. Bull. 23:1047–1055.

Kallman, H., et al., eds. 1987. Restoring America's wildlife 1937-1987. U.S. Fish and Wildl. Serv., Washington, D.C. 394 pp.

Karr, J. R., and R. R. Roth. 1971. Vegetation structure and avian diversity in several New World areas. Am. Nat. 105:423-435.

Kerpez, T. A., and N. S. Smith. 1990. Competition between European starlings and native woodpeckers for nest cavities in saguaros. Auk 107:367-375.

Kim, J. T., T. J. Grizzard, L. W. Randall, and R. C. Hoehn. 1978. Urban runoff and the stream life of the Occoquan. Pages 155-160 *in* The freshwater Potomac: aquatic communities and environmental stresses. Tech. Pub. 78-2. Interstate Commission on the Potomac River Basin, Rockville, Maryland.

Klein, R. D. 1979. Urbanization and stream quality impairment. Water Resour. Bull. 15:948-963.

Klem, D., Jr. 1991. Glass and bird kills: an overview and suggested planning and design methods of preventing a fatal hazard. Pages 99-103 *in* L. W. Adams and D. L. Leedy, eds. Wildlife conservation in metropolitan environments. Natl. Inst. for Urban Wildl., Columbia, Maryland.

Knight, J. E. 1983. Jackrabbits. Pages D-75 through D-80 *in* R. M. Timm, ed. Prevention and control of wildlife damage. Great Plains Agric. Council Wildl. Resour. Comm. and Nebraska Coop. Ext. Serv., Univ. Nebraska, Lincoln.

Kolb, H. H. 1985. Habitat use by foxes in Edinburgh. Terre Vie 40:139-143.

Kowarik, I. 1990. Some responses of flora and vegetation to urbanization in central Europe. Pages 45-74 *in* H. Sukopp, S. Hejny, and I. Kowarik, eds. Urban ecology: plants and plant communities in urban environments. SPB Acad. Publ. bv, The Hague, The Netherlands.

Lancaster, R. K., and W. E. Rees. 1979. Bird communities and the structure of urban habitats. Can. J. Zool. 57:2358-2368.

Landsberg, H. E. 1981. The urban climate. Academic Press, New York. 275 pp.

Laux, L. J., Jr., J. F. Gallagher, and S. Dubs. 1991. Nesting of the American crow in urban areas. Page 247 *in* L. W. Adams and D. L. Leedy, eds. Wildlife conservation in metropolitan environments. Natl. Inst. for Urban Wildl., Columbia, Maryland.

Leedy, D. L., and L. W. Adams. 1984. A guide to urban wildlife management. Natl. Inst. for Urban Wildl., Columbia, Maryland. 42 pp.

Leedy, D. L., R. M. Maestro, and T. M. Franklin. 1978. Planning for wildlife in cities and suburbs. Rep. No. FWS/OBS-77/66. U.S. Fish and Wildl. Serv., Washington, D.C. 64 pp.

Leopold, A. 1933. Game management. Charles Scribner's Sons, New York. 481 pp.

Leopold, A. 1949. A sand county almanac and sketches here and there. Oxford Univ. Press, New York. 226 pp.

Leopold, A. 1953. Round river. Ed. L. B. Leopold. Oxford Univ. Press, New York. 173 pp.

Leopold, A. S., and M. F. Dedon. 1983. Resident mourning doves in Berkeley, California. J. Wildl. Manage. 47:780-789.

Levesque, H., and R. McNeil. 1986. Movement of rock doves *(Columba livia)* in the old section of Montreal harbor. (in French, English abstract). Naturaliste Can. (Rev. Ecol. Syst.) 113:47-54.

Linduska, J. P. 1987. Wood duck domain: the coastal plain. Pages 89-103 *in* H. Kallman, et al., eds. Restoring America's wildlife 1937-1987. U.S. Fish and Wildl. Serv., Washington, D.C.

Luniak, M. 1983. The avifauna of urban green areas in Poland and possibilities of managing it. Acta Ornithologica 19:3-61.

Lynch, T. E., and D. W. Speake. 1978. Eastern wild turkey behavioral responses induced by sonic boom. Pages 47-61 *in* J. L. Fletcher and R. G. Busnel, eds. Effects of noise on wildlife. Academic Press, Inc., New York.

MacArthur, R. H., and J. W. MacArthur. 1961. On bird species diversity. Ecology 42:594-598.

168   References

MacArthur, R. H., and E. O. Wilson. 1967. The theory of island biogeography. Princeton Univ. Press, Princeton, New Jersey. 203 pp.

MacClintock, L., R. F. Whitcomb, and B. L. Whitcomb. 1977. Evidence for the value of corridors and minimization of isolation in preservation of biotic diversity. Am. Birds 31:6-16.

MacCracken, J. G. 1982. Coyote foods in a southern California suburb. Wildl. Soc. Bull. 10:280-281.

Manski, D. A., and J. M. Hadidian. 1987. Raccoon ecology in and adjacent to an urban national park. Page 237 in L. W. Adams and D. L. Leedy, eds. Integrating man and nature in the metropolitan environment. Natl. Inst. for Urban Wildl., Columbia, Maryland.

Manski, D. A., L. W. VanDruff, and V. Flyger. 1981. Activities of gray squirrels and people in a downtown Washington, D.C. park: management implications. Trans. North Am. Wildl. and Nat. Resour. Conf. 46:439-454.

Martin, A. C., H. S. Zim, and A. L. Nelson. [1951] 1961. American wildlife & plants: a guide to wildlife food habits. Dover Publ., Inc., New York. 500 pp.

Master, T. L., and C. S. Oplinger. 1984. Nesting and brood rearing ecology of an urban waterfowl population (*Anas platyrhynchos* and *Branta canadensis*) in Allentown, Pennsylvania. Proc. Pa. Acad. Sci. 58:175-180.

McAninch, J. B., and J. M. Parker. 1991. Urban deer management programs: a facilitated approach. Trans. North Am. Wildl. and Nat. Resour. Conf. 56:428-436.

Meier, K. E. 1983. Habitat use by opossums in an urban environment. M.S. thesis, Oregon State Univ., Corvallis. 69 pp.

Middleton, N. C. 1984. Fame comes to Roanoke's "STP" as stopover for transients. Raven 53:43-47.

Miller, J. E. 1983a. Beavers. Pages B-1 through B-11 in R. M. Timm, ed. Prevention and control of wildlife damage. Great Plains Agric. Council Wildl. Resour. Comm. and Nebraska Coop. Ext. Serv., Univ. Nebraska, Lincoln.

Miller, J. E. 1983b. Muskrats. Pages B-51 through B-59 in R. M. Timm, ed. Prevention and control of wildlife damage. Great Plains Agric. Council Wildl. Resour. Comm. and Nebraska Coop. Ext. Serv., Univ. Nebraska, Lincoln.

Mills, G. S., J. B. Dunning, Jr., and J. M. Bates. 1989. Effects of urbanization on breeding bird community structure in southwestern desert habitats. Condor 91:416-428.

Minton, S. A., Jr. 1968. The fate of amphibians and reptiles in a suburban area. J. Herpetology 2:113-116.

Mitchell, R. T. 1986. Urban insects II: butterflies in your garden. Urban Wildlife Manager's Notebook—11. Natl. Inst. for Urban Wildl., Columbia, Maryland. 6 pp.

Moore, J. C. 1956. Observations of manatees in aggregations. Am. Mus. Novit. 1811:1-24.

Moran, M. A. 1984. Influence of adjacent land use on understory vegetation of New York forests. Urban Ecol. 8:329-340.

Morgan, M. D., and K. R. Philipp. 1986. The effect of agricultural and residential development on aquatic macrophytes in the New Jersey Pine Barrens. Biol. Conserv. 35:143-158.

Morris, A. A. 1989. Jamaica Bay wildlife refuge. Birder's World, August, pp. 42-46.

Morrison, J., and P. Williams. 1988. Warm Springs marsh restoration. Pages 340-349 in J. A. Kusler, S. Daly, and G. Brooks, eds. Urban wetlands: proceedings of the national wetland symposium. Assoc. of Wetland Managers, Berne, New York.

Murphy, D. D. 1988. Challenges to biological diversity in urban areas. Pages 71-76 in E. O. Wilson, ed. Biodiversity. Natl. Acad. Press, Washington, D.C.

Myers, N. 1988. Tropical forests and their species: going, going . . . ? Pages 28-35 in E. O. Wilson, ed. Biodiversity. Natl. Acad. Press, Washington, D.C.

Nelson, H. K., and R. B. Oetting. 1982. An overview of management of Canada geese (*Branta canadensis*) and their adaptation to suburban conditions in the USA. Aquila 89:303-306.

Niering, W. A., and R. H. Goodwin. 1974. Creation of relatively stable shrublands with herbicides: arresting "succession" rights-of-way and pastureland. Ecology 55:784-795.

Noss, R. F. 1987. Protecting natural areas in fragmented landscapes. Nat. Areas J. 7:2-13.

Noss, R. F., and L. D. Harris. 1986. Nodes, networks, and MUMs: preserving diversity at all scales. Environ. Manage. 10:299-309.

Obrecht, H. H., III., W. J. Fleming, and J. H. Parsons. 1991. Management of powerline rights-of-way for botanical and wildlife value in metropolitan areas. Page 255 *in* L. W. Adams and D. L. Leedy, eds. Wildlife conservation in metropolitan environments. Natl. Inst. for Urban Wildl., Columbia, Maryland.

Odum, E. P. 1971. Fundamentals of ecology. 3rd ed. W B Saunders Co., Philadelphia, Pennsylvania. 574 pp.

OECD. 1986. Control of water pollution from urban run-off. Environ. Monogr. 3. Org. for Econ. Co-op. and Dev., Paris, France. 96 pp.

Oetting, R. B. 1987. Some management strategies for resident Canada geese. Paper presented at 54th annual meeting of the Assoc. of Midwest Fish and Wildl. Agencies, 15-16 July, Winnipeg, Manitoba. Typescript.

Oke, T. R. 1973. City size and the urban heat island. Atmospheric Environment 7:769-779.

Oliphant, L. W., and E. Haug. 1985. Productivity, population density and rate of increase of an expanding merlin population. Raptor Res. 19:56-59.

Oliphant, L. W., and S. McTaggart. 1977. Prey utilized by urban merlins. The Can. Field-Nat. 91:190-192.

Orser, P. N., and D. J. Shure. 1972. Effects of urbanization on the salamander *Desmognathus fuscus fuscus*. Ecology 53:1148-1154.

O'Shea, T. J. 1987. The past, present, and future of manatees in the southeastern United States: realities, misunderstandings and enigmas. Pages 184-204 *in* R. R. Odom, K. A. Riddleberger, and J. C. Ozier, eds. Proceedings of the third southeastern nongame and endangered wildlife symposium. Georgia Dept. Nat. Resour., Social Circle.

Owen, D. F. 1978. Insect diversity in an English suburban garden. Pages 13-29 *in* G. W. Frankie and C. S. Koehler, eds. Perspectives in urban entomology. Academic Press, New York.

Parker, J. W. 1987. Urban-nesting Mississippi kites: history, problems, management, and benefits. Pages 233-234 *in* L. W. Adams and D. L. Leedy, eds. Integrating man and nature in the metropolitan environment. Natl. Inst. for Urban Wildl., Columbia, Maryland.

Peach, W. J., and J. A. Fowler. 1989. Movements of wing-tagged starlings *Sturnus vulgaris* from an urban communal roost in winter. Bird Study 36:16-22.

Penland, S. T. 1984. Avian responses to a gradient of urbanization in Seattle, Washington. Ph.D. dissertation, Univ. Washington, Seattle. 407 pp.

Peterson, A. T. 1986. Rock doves nesting in trees. Wilson Bull. 98:168-169.

Pet Food Institute. 1990. Pet Food Institute fact sheet 1990. Pet Food Inst., Washington, D.C. Typescript.

Pfeifer, W. K. 1983. Waterfowl. Pages E-75 through E-78 *in* R. M. Timm, ed. Prevention and control of wildlife damage. Great Plains Agric. Council Wildl. Resour. Comm. and Nebraska Coop. Ext. Serv., Univ. Nebraska, Lincoln.

Pickering, J. R., and R. G. Perkins. 1982. Planting frequencies and trends of street trees in southern Ontario municipalities. J. Arboriculture 8:189-192.

Piest, L. A., and L. K. Sowls. 1985. Breeding duck use of a sewage marsh in Arizona. J. Wildl. Manage. 49:580-585.

Polsley, R. 1975. Hunger, prey feeding, and predatory aggression. Behav. Biol. 13:81-93.

Prescott, K. W. 1985. Eastern screech-owl captures goldfish in patio pond. Wilson Bull. 97:572-573.

Profous, G. V., and R. E. Loeb. 1984. Vegetation and plant communities of Van Cortlandt Park, Bronx, New York. Bull. Torrey Bot. Club 111:80-89.

Quinn, T. 1991. Distribution and habitat associations of coyotes in Seattle, Washington. Pages 47-51 in L. W. Adams and D. L. Leedy, eds. Wildlife conservation in metropolitan environments. Natl. Inst. for Urban Wildl., Columbia, Maryland.

Reaume, R. F. 1986. Watercourse treatment in high density residential development. Pages 100-101 in K. Stenberg and W. W. Shaw, eds. Wildlife conservation and new residential developments. School of Renewable Nat. Resour., Univ. Arizona, Tucson.

Record, C. R. 1983. Franklin, Richardson and Columbian ground squirrels. Pages B-133 through B-136 in R. M. Timm, ed. Prevention and control of wildlife damage. Great Plains Agric. Council Wildl. Resour. Comm. and Nebraska Coop. Ext. Serv., Univ. Nebraska, Lincoln.

Reethof, G., and G. M. Heisler. 1976. Trees and forests for noise abatement and visual screening. Pages 39-48 in F. S. Santamour, Jr., H. D. Gerhold, and S. Little, eds. Better trees for metropolitan landscapes. USDA For. Serv. Gen. Tech. Rep. NE-22. U.S. Gov. Print. Off., Washington, D.C.

Rhoads, A. F., P. W. Meyer, and R. Sanfelippo. 1981. Performance of urban street trees evaluated. J. Arboriculture 7:127-132.

Robbins, C. S. 1991. Managing suburban forest fragments for birds. Pages 253-264 in D. J. Decker et al., eds. Challenges in the conservation of biological resources: a practitioner's guide. Westview Press, Boulder, Colorado.

Robel, R. J. 1961. Water depth and turbidity in relation to growth of sago pondweed. J. Wildl. Manage. 25:436-438.

Robinson, W. L., and E. G. Bolen. 1989. Wildlife ecology and management. 2nd ed. Macmillan Publishing Co., New York. 574 pp.

Rosatte, R. C., P. M. Kelly-Ward, and C. D. MacInnes. 1987. A strategy for controlling rabies in urban skunks and raccoons. Pages 161-167 in L. W. Adams and D. L. Leedy, eds. Integrating man and nature in the metropolitan environment. Natl. Inst. for Urban Wildl., Columbia, Maryland.

Roth, R. R. 1987. Assessment of habitat quality for wood thrush in a residential area. Pages 139-149 in L. W. Adams and D. L. Leedy, eds. Integrating man and nature in the metropolitan environment. Natl. Inst. for Urban Wildl., Columbia, Maryland.

Rowntree, R. A. 1984a. Ecology of the urban forest. Urban Ecol. 8:1-11.

Rowntree, R. A. 1984b. Forest canopy cover and land use in four eastern United States cities. Urban Ecol. 8:55-67.

Rowntree, R. A., and R. A. Sanders. 1981. The urban forest resource. New York State Forest Resour. Assessment Rep. No. 13. USDA For. Serv., State Univ. New York, Syracuse. 99 pp.

Ruckel, S. W. 1987. The status of the American alligator in Georgia. Pages 91-97 in R. R. Odom, K. A. Riddleberger, and J. C. Ozier, eds. Proceedings of the third southeastern nongame and endangered wildlife symposium. Georgia Dept. Nat. Resour., Social Circle.

Ruff, A. R. 1987. Holland and the ecological landscapes 1973-1987. Delft Univ. Press, Delft, The Netherlands. 120 pp.

Ryan, D. A., and J. S. Larson. 1976. Chipmunks in residential environments. Urban Ecology 2:173-178.

San Julian, G. J., H. A. Phillips, R. B. Hazel, and D. T. Harke. 1984. North Carolina animal damage control manual. North Carolina Agric. Ext. Serv., Raleigh.

Sargeant, A. B., S. H. Allen, and R. T. Eberhardt. 1984. Red fox predation on breeding ducks in midcontinent North America. Wildl. Monogr. No. 89. 41 pp.

Sargeant, A. B., S. H. Allen, and J. O. Hastings. 1987. Spatial relations between sympatric coyotes and red foxes in North Dakota. J. Wildl. Manage. 51:285-293.

Schicker, L. 1987. Design criteria for children and wildlife in residential developments. Pages 99-105 *in* L. W. Adams and D. L. Leedy, eds. Integrating man and nature in the metropolitan environment. Natl. Inst. for Urban Wildl., Columbia, Maryland.

Schinner, J. R., and D. L. Cauley. 1974. The ecology of urban raccoons in Cincinnati, Ohio. Pages 125-130 *in* J. H. Noyes and D. R. Progulske, eds. Wildlife in an urbanizing environment. Plan. and Resour. Dev. Series No. 28. Holdsworth Natural Resources Center, Univ. Massachusetts, Amherst.

Schlauch, F. C. 1978. Urban geographical ecology of the amphibians and reptiles of Long Island. Pages 25-41 *in* C. M. Kirkpatrick, ed. Wildlife and people. Purdue Res. Found., West Lafayette, Indiana.

Shargo, E. S. 1988. Home range, movements, and activity patterns of coyotes *(Canis latrans)* in Los Angeles suburbs. Ph.D. dissertation, Univ. California, Los Angeles. 113 pp.

Shaw, W. W., J. M. Burns, and K. Stenberg. 1986. Wildlife habitats in Tucson: a strategy for conservation. School of Renewable Nat. Resour., Univ. Arizona, Tucson. 17 pp.

Shellhammer, H. S. 1989. Salt marsh harvest mice, urban development, and rising sea levels. Conserv. Biol. 3:59-65.

Shoesmith, M. W., and W. H. Koonz. 1977. The maintenance of an urban deer herd in Winnipeg, Manitoba. Trans. North Am. Wildl. and Nat. Resour. Conf. 42:278-285.

Singer, M. C., and L. E. Gilbert. 1978. Ecology of butterflies in the urbs and suburbs. Pages 1-11 *in* G. W. Frankie and C. S. Koehler, eds. Perspectives in urban entomology. Academic Press, New York.

Slate, D. 1985. Movement, activity and home range patterns among members of a high density suburban raccoon population. Ph.D. dissertation, State Univ. New Jersey, Rutgers. 112 pp.

Smardon, R. C. 1988. Perception and aesthetics of the urban environment: review of the role of vegetation. Landscape and Urban Planning 15:85-106.

Smith, D. G., and R. Gilbert. 1984. Eastern screech-owl home range and use of suburban habitats in southern Connecticut. J. Field Ornithol. 55:322-329.

Smith, W. G. 1982. Water quality enhancement through stormwater detention. Pages 236-244 *in* W. DeGroot, ed. Stormwater detention facilities. Am. Soc. of Civil Eng., New York.

Soulé, M. E., et al. 1988. Reconstructed dynamics of rapid extinctions of chaparral-requiring birds in urban habitat islands. Conserv. Biol. 2:75-92.

Spirn, A. W. 1984. The granite garden: urban nature and human design. Basic Books, New York.

Stevenson, G. M., Jr. 1972. Noise and the urban environment. Pages 195-228 *in* T. R. Detwyler and M. G. Marcus, eds. Urbanization and environment. Duxbury Press, Belmont, California.

Stickley, A. R., Jr., D. J. Twedt, J. F. Heisterberg, D. F. Mott, and J. F. Glahn. 1986. Surfactant spray system for controlling blackbirds and starlings in urban roosts. Wildl. Soc. Bull. 14:412-418.

Sukopp, H., and S. Weiler. 1988. Biotope mapping and nature conservation strategies in urban areas of the Federal Republic of Germany. Landscape and Urban Planning 15:39-58.

Swanson, G. A. 1977. Diel food selection by Anatinae on a waste-stabilization system. J. Wildl. Manage. 41:226-231.

Thomas, J. W., and R. A. Dixon. 1974. Cemetery ecology. Pages 107-110 *in* J. H. Noyes and D. R. Progulske, eds. Wildlife in an urbanizing environment. Plann. and Resour. Dev. Ser. 28. Holdsworth Natural Resources Center, Univ. Massachusetts, Amherst.

Thompson, D. C., and P. S. Thompson. 1980. Food habits and caching behavior of urban gray squirrels. Can. J. Zool. 58:701-710.

Thompson, D. Q., R. L. Stuckey, and E. B. Thompson. 1987. Spread, impact, and control of purple loosestrife *(Lythrum salicaria)* in North American wetlands. Fish and Wildlife Research 2. U.S. Fish and Wildl. Serv., Washington, D.C. 55 pp.

Tilghman, N. G. 1987. Characteristics of urban woodlands affecting breeding bird diversity and abundance. Landscape and Urban Planning 14:481-495.

Tilghman, N. G. 1989. Impacts of white-tailed deer on forest regeneration in northwestern Pennsylvania. J. Wildl. Manage. 53:524-532.

Tiner, R. W., Jr. 1984. Wetlands of the United States: current status and recent trends. U.S. Dept. of the Inter., Fish and Wildl. Serv., Washington, D.C. 59 pp.

Trippensee, R. E. 1948. Wildlife management. Vol. I. Upland game and general principles. McGraw-Hill Book Co., Inc., New York. 479 pp.

Trippensee, R. E. 1953. Wildlife management. Vol. II. Furbearers, waterfowl, and fish. McGraw-Hill Book Co., Inc., New York. 572 pp.

Turner, J. W., Jr., I. K. M. Liu, and J. F. Kirkpatrick. 1992. Remotely delivered immunocontraception in captive white-tailed deer. J. Wildl. Manage. 56:154-157.

Tweit, R. C., and J. C. Tweit. 1986. Urban development effects on the abundance of some common resident birds of the Tucson area of Arizona. Am. Birds 40:431-436.

Ulrich, R. S. 1979. Visual landscape and psychological well-being. Landscape Res. 4:17-23.

U.S. Bureau of the Census. 1991. Statistical abstract of the United States: 1991. 111th edition. U.S. Bureau of the Census, Washington, D.C.

U.S. Fish and Wildlife Service. 1988. 1985 national survey of hunting, fishing, and wildlife-associated recreation. U.S. Gov. Print. Off., Washington, D.C. 167 pp.

van der Zande, A. N., et al. 1984. Impact of outdoor recreation on the density of a number of breeding bird species in woods adjacent to urban residential areas. Biol. Conserv. 30:1-39.

VanDruff, L. W. 1979. Urban wildlife—neglected resource. Pages 184-190 *in* R. Teague and E. Decker, eds. Wildlife conservation: principles and practices. The Wildl. Soc., Washington, D.C.

VanDruff, L. W., and R. N. Rowse. 1986. Habitat association of mammals in Syracuse, New York. Urban Ecol. 9:413-434.

Vink, A. P. A. 1983. Landscape ecology and land use. Longman Inc., New York. 264 pp.

Vizyová, A. 1986. Urban woodlots as islands for land vertebrates: a preliminary attempt on estimating the barrier effects of urban structural units. Ecology (CSSR) 5:407-419.

Walcott, C. F. 1974. Changes in bird life in Cambridge, Massachusetts from 1860 to 1964. Auk 91:151-160.

Weber, W. 1979. Pigeon-associated people diseases. Proc. Bird Control Seminar 8:156-158.

Wegner, J. F., and G. Merriam. 1979. Movements by birds and small mammals between a wood and adjoining farmland habitats. J. Appl. Ecol. 16:349-357.

Weller, M. W. 1987. Freshwater marshes: ecology and wildlife management. 2nd ed. Univ. Minnesota Press, Minneapolis. 150 pp.

Wesemann, T., and M. Rowe. 1987. Factors influencing the distribution and abundance of burrowing owls in Cape Coral, Florida. Pages 129-137 *in* L. W. Adams and D. L. Leedy, eds. Integrating man and nature in the metropolitan environment. Natl. Inst. for Urban Wildl., Columbia, Maryland.

Westemeier, R. L., and W. R. Edwards. 1987. Prairie-chickens: survival in the midwest. Pages 119-131 *in* H. Kallman, ed. Restoring America's wildlife 1937-1987. U.S. Fish and Wildl. Serv., Washington, D.C.

Whitcomb, R. F., et al. 1981. Effects of forest fragmentation on avifauna of the eastern deciduous forest. Pages 125-205 *in* R. L. Burgess and D. M. Sharpe, eds. Forest island dynamics in man-dominated landscapes. Springer-Verlag, New York.

Whitney, G. G., and S. D. Adams. 1980. Man as a maker of new plant communities. J. Applied Ecol. 17:431-448.

Williams, O., and J. McKegg. 1987. Nuisance furbearer management programs for urban areas. Pages 156-163 *in* M. Novak, J. A. Baker, M. E. Obbard, and B. Malloch, eds. Wild furbearer management and conservation in North America. Ontario Trappers Assoc., North Bay, Canada.

Williamson, R. D. 1983. Identification of urban habitat components which affect eastern gray squirrel abundance. Urban Ecol. 7:345-356.

Wilson, E. O. 1984. Biophilia. Harvard Univ. Press, Cambridge, Massachusetts. 157 pp.

Witham, J. H., and J. M. Jones. 1990. White-tailed deer abundance on metropolitan forest preserves during winter in northeastern Illinois. Wildl. Soc. Bull. 18:13-16.

Woodward, A. R., D. N. David, and T. C. Hines. 1987. American alligator management in Florida. Pages 98-113 *in* R. R. Odom, K. A. Riddleberger, and J. C. Ozier, eds. Proceedings of the third southeastern nongame and endangered wildlife symposium. Georgia Dept. Nat. Resour., Social Circle.

Wright, D. H. 1990. Human impacts on energy flow through natural ecosystems and implications for species endangerment. Ambio 19:189-194.

Yahner, R. H. 1987. Habitat features affecting burrow-site selection by eastern chipmunks in a campus landscape in central Pennsylvania. Proc. Penn. Acad. Sci. 61:174-176.

Yoakum, J., et al. 1980. Habitat improvement techniques. Pages 329-403 *in* S. D. Schemnitz, ed. Wildlife management techniques manual. The Wildl. Soc., Washington, D.C.

Youngberg, R. J. 1983. Shading effects of deciduous trees. J. Arboriculture 9:295-297.

Yurus, J. 1986. Song dog in the suburbs. Animal Kingdom 89:35-39.

Zeleny, L. 1976. The bluebird. Indiana Univ. Press, Bloomington. 170 pp.

Zentner, J. 1988. Wetland restoration in urbanized areas: examples from coastal California. Pages 310-312 *in* J. A. Kusler, S. Daly, and G. Brooks, eds. Urban wetlands: proceedings of the national wetland symposium. Assoc. of Wetland Managers, Berne, New York.

Index

175

Lowell W. Adams is vice president of the National Institute for Urban Wildlife in Columbia, Maryland. He received his Ph.D. in wildlife biology and has studied urban habitats and their associated wildlife communities for over 15 years. Dr. Adams also is a part-time faculty member of the University of Maryland and of Johns Hopkins University, where he teaches courses in wildlife ecology and management. He is senior author of *Wildlife Reserves and Corridors in the Urban Environment* and senior editor of *Integrating Man and Nature in the Metropolitan Environment* and *Wildlife Conservation in Metropolitan Environments*.